Jesus: Fib, Dead, or God?

James Finke

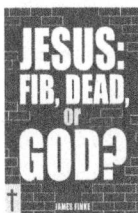

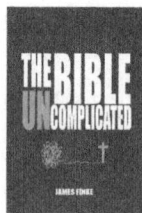

This book gives the business case for why we believe the Bible is the Word of God. Are you ready? Let's talk Bible.

***

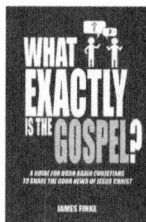

This book shares the most powerful message ever delivered on planet Earth. Let's talk Gospel.

JAMES FINKE READERS' CLUB

My free monthly email newsletter is packed with useful info to help you share the Good News of Jesus Christ with others. It contains deals and giveaways that aren't offered anywhere else, and you'll be the first to hear when new books in the series are released!

Subscribers receive a welcome package that includes:

1. A free book of mine that is ONLY available to my readers' club.

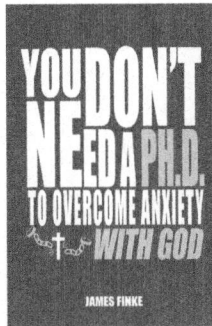

2. A free audio download of the "You Don't Need a Ph.D. to Find G-O-D" message I delivered at my home church.

SUBSCRIBE

Contents

INTRODUCTION

It was by the grace of God that my wife and I purchased our house back in 2014. The sellers were notoriously difficult to work with and had chased off multiple prospective buyers before we ever got involved. As a result, the property had been vacant for over a year by the time we bought it. While the house was still in good shape, the above-ground pool most certainly was not. What was once a beautiful backyard oasis was now a dilapidated mess. The main deck had partially collapsed, the catwalk around the pool had rotted out, and the equipment was in shambles.

We hired a pool company to help revamp our oasis. They replaced the damaged equipment and set us up with a new pump, filter, and connecting hoses. They removed the filthy old pool liner and replaced it with a crisp new blue one. Next, we brought in a contractor who took down the collapsed deck and built a beautiful new one in its place. As for the catwalk, our contractor was concerned that he'd damage the pool if he tried to remove it, so we agreed to add a new layer on top rather than risk the damage. We were determined to have the pool ready for our daughter's birthday party, so this would do the job for now. We could always replace it down the road if need be.

With a new layer of decking covering up the rotted catwalk, we had what looked like a brand-new pool. All we needed now was to fill it up. So, one fine morning, the water delivery truck rolled up. On said day, our family came out and watched as they pumped thousands of gallons of water into the pool. We were so excited; the kids would be swimming before they knew it.

The first truckload filled up the pool about ¾ of the way. It would be a couple of hours before the water guys could return with another truckload to top us off, so, in the meantime, I headed into the office to get some work done. I had no idea of the turn the day was about to take.

I got a call from my wife a couple of hours later. I expected to hear splashing and laughing in the background, but as soon as I heard the tone of her voice, I knew something was wrong. Shortly after the delivery guys topped off the pool with the second truckload of water, one of the walls buckled. Water was everywhere, and they were pumping out what little was left to try to prevent the entire pool from collapsing. We were shocked.

I'll spare you the details of the entire ordeal, but we learned that the rotted catwalk was not just a decorative feature that could be covered up. Rather, it was an integral part of the pool's structural integrity. Without this decking intact, the pool cannot withstand the weight it's designed to hold and is virtually useless. **We had spent so much time and energy addressing secondary aspects of the pool that we missed the very foundation of the structure.**

It's not that we should have ignored the other components, but without the structural integrity, they crumbled under the weight of the water. What good is a new filter if the pool can't hold water? What good is a new liner if the wall it's connected to collapses?

After the collapse, we shifted our focus away from the ancillary issues and lasered in on the structural integrity. Only once we determined the foundation was solid did we move on to address the other components.

It was a costly but valuable lesson to learn because the principle applies broadly in our lives. Consider how this principle applies to a matter with *eternal* consequences. **Many of us spend so much time and energy wrestling with ancillary issues that we miss the very foundation of the Christian faith**. So, let's get right to it. Whether you're examining your own faith or answering questions from someone else, the bottom line is this:

If Jesus rose from the dead, Christianity is true.

If the resurrection is false, well... I can't state it any more plainly than the Apostle Paul does in the Bible: "And if Christ has not been raised, our preaching is useless and so is your faith." [1]

The structural integrity of our faith is built upon a historical event – the resurrection of Jesus. Therefore, it only makes sense to move on

---

1. 1 Cor 15:14

to the other components once we've determined the resurrection is true. That's precisely the approach we'll take together throughout this book.

Today, we joke that our house may go down if a tornado comes through, but that pool is so fortified that it will still be standing. If I do my job with this book, you'll see that no matter what storms shake your life, your faith will remain standing if you build it on the absolute truth of the resurrection of Jesus.

Are you ready? Let's talk Christianity.

***

PART 1: THE STRUCTURAL INTEGRITY OF OUR FAITH

Chapter 1

SPIRITUAL WHAC-A-MOLE

THE STRUCTURAL INTEGRITY OF OUR FAITH

For perhaps the first time ever, I was excited to go to my 6-month teeth cleaning appointment. I was looking forward to gifting copies of my first book (You Don't Need a Ph.D. to Find G-O-D) to my hygienist and my dentist.

As I explained what the book is about to my hygienist, her eyes lit up. It turns out her 17-year-old brother had been questioning his faith, so much so that their Mom felt his unbelief was damaging the entire family. She also has two young kids asking certain questions about God that she didn't feel equipped to answer. She needed precisely the type of answers that a book like this could provide. I really can't make it up. Only God could use a dentist appointment for His glory.

Now, onto my dentist. Dr. C is a wonderful guy who has taken care of multiple generations of my family. As is his custom, he came into the room to check up on me toward the end of the cleaning. I couldn't say much since I had multiple dental utensils in my mouth, but eventually, we got to chat. I gave him his copy of the book with a personal note on the inside of the cover. It was a special moment, and he asked about the topic of the book. I explained that it was Christian Apologetics, meaning it provides a rational defense of the Christian faith.

What ensued from there is something I call *Spiritual Whac-A-Mole*. Have you ever played that carnival game called Whac-A-Mole? The player holds a large, soft mallet and stands over the play area. Plastic "moles" randomly pop their heads up out of holes in the play area. Points are scored by hitting the moles with the mallet as they pop up. As soon as you hit one mole, another immediately pops up in a different spot. If you don't whack the mole within a certain amount of time, it goes back down into its hole, and no score is earned. As a carnival game, it's great. As a method to discuss our faith in the living God... less great.

For about 10 minutes, Dr. C respectfully questioned everything from the reliability of the Bible, to the exclusivity of Jesus' claims, to same-sex marriage, to hypocrites in the church, to the crusades, and more – all this as I sat in the dentist's chair. As soon as I addressed one issue, another popped its head out in a different spot. As soon as I handled that one, there was another, and so forth. Hence, Spiritual Whac-A-Mole. Can you picture it?

Pop: Can we really trust a book that was written 2,000 years ago? Pop: But it's been translated so many times. Pop: Didn't Jesus' followers try to make their religion attractive by adding mythology to His life? Pop: I think some Christians use their beliefs to justify prejudice. Pop: I can't understand why an athlete would thank God during a game. Doesn't God have better things to do? Pop: We have homosexual patients who are some of the nicest people you'll meet. And think of how many heterosexuals are horrible parents. Pop: It seems like some Christians are hypocrites. Pop: Isn't it arrogant to believe Jesus is the only way to heaven? **Pop, Pop, Pop, Pop, Pop**.

Unfortunately, there's no stuffed animal prize at the end of this type of Whac-A-Mole. Dr. C's objections were sincere. It was clear he had wrestled with these issues personally. They were worthy of discussion and clarification. But it clicked to me when we finally got to the crux of the issue. Dr. C seemed very comfortable with the idea that Jesus was a wise and enlightened moral teacher, but he did not yet accept Him as the Son of God. Suddenly, the litany of issues we had discussed seemed totally misdirected. They made for great conversation, but I thought for a moment, *if Jesus isn't the Son of God, what are we talking about here?* The takeaway is this:

It's out of order to delve into Bible translations, or hypocritical Christians, or [insert ancillary issue] before discussing whether the resurrection is true.

It's about as prudent as picking out paint colors for a house that might have a crumbling foundation.

The Bible instructs us to share the Good News of Jesus Christ with all nations. That means every Christian is bound to interact with people who have sincere objections, concerns, and questions about the faith. We ought to be prepared to explain why we believe. Jesus Himself said He sends out His followers "like sheep among wolves."[1]

We must also wrestle with our own questions and doubts. We're instructed to "Love the Lord your God with all your heart and with all your soul and with all your **mind**." [2] If we're going to do that effectively, it starts with the foundation. If Christianity hinges on the life, death, and resurrection of Jesus Christ, it stands to reason that the baseline for discussion would very simply be: **who is Jesus**? Let's explore that question.

***

---

1. Matthew 10:16

2. Matthew 22:37, emphasis mine.

Chapter 2

FIB, DEAD, OR GOD?

*"When Jesus came into the region of Caesarea Phillipi, He asked His disciples, 'Who do men say that I, the Son of Man, am?' So, they said, 'Some say John the Baptist, some, Elijah, and others, Jeremiah or one of the prophets.' He said to them, 'But who do **you** say that I am?'"*[1]

Who do you say that I am? Nearly two thousand years have passed since Jesus posed this question to his disciples. Yet, it remains the most important question in history as Jesus remains the most important person in history. The classic essay, One Solitary Life sums it up: "I am far within the mark when I say that all the armies that

---

1. Matthew 16:13-15, emphasis mine.

ever marched, all the navies that were ever built, all the parliaments that ever sat and all the kings that ever reigned, put together, have not affected the life of man upon this earth as powerfully as that one solitary life."[2]

So... who is He?

If you were to poll a hundred people, you might get a hundred different answers. In his book, "The Case for the Real Jesus," Lee Strobel details a poll taken by Newsweek around Christmas 2006. He highlights some eye-opening responses to the question, "Who is Jesus?" I've paraphrased several of them here: [3]

1. He exists for those who want him to exist.

2. A legend.

3. A myth.

4. About as real as Santa Claus.

5. About as real as the Tooth Fairy.

6. A fairy tale for grown-ups.

7. Invisible man in the sky.

8. A caricature.

---

2. James Allen Francis. *One Solitary Life.*

3. Lee Strobel, *The Case for the Real Jesus* (Grand Rapids, Michigan: Zondervan, 2007), 10.

9. There was no Jesus.

10. I don't care. It doesn't affect me.

11. A rabbi who is an example of compassion. Since then, he has been exploited by Christians, particularly Americans.

12. A liberal.

13. One of a thousand Jews murdered by the Romans for threatening Roman rule.

14. Everyman. Too bad he was in male form this time around.

15. An enlightened being.

16. A man nailed to a tree for saying how great it would be to be nice to people for a change.

17. A highly moral person. No more, no less.

18. Jesus died disappointed. Anything more is fantasy.

19. Bipolar and schizophrenic.

20. A prophet who made a wrong bet and should be ignored.

Spoiler alert: Not one of these responses aligns with what the Bible actually teaches us about Jesus. Some deny His existence altogether. Others focus on one particular trait or aspect of His being. For instance, he is an "example of compassion." That's great, but I don't believe we would put our faith in and worship a first-century carpenter because He's "an example of compassion." So, we should quit on our recurring theme of focusing on the periphery and missing the main point. Instead, we need to get to the heart of the matter, and I submit to you a tool to do just that:

Fib, Dead, or God?

As diverse as they may sound on the surface, I'm convinced that views of Jesus generally fall into three categories:

- **Fib**: Jesus is a lie. He never existed as a human being.

- **Dead**: Jesus, the man, existed, but he was just a man, not God (therefore, he's dead).

- **God**: Jesus, the man, exists, and He is who He claimed to be – God in the flesh.

Fib: This is the belief that Jesus outright never existed. I classify responses #1-10 to this group if you refer back to the Newsweek list. It may sound crazy to outright deny His existence (it is), but then again, there are people out there who believe all sorts of wild conspiracy theories.

The gist of the theory (called mythicism) is that if Jesus existed, you would expect Him to be mentioned more in non-Biblical first-century writings. There are also derivatives of the theory claiming that Christians incorrectly added Jesus to various first-century writings outside of the Bible.

Just so I'm clear, this theory basically says, other than this robust collection of reliable historical documents called the Bible, first century texts didn't mention Jesus as often as you'd expect. That's quite the qualifier.

We're going to dive into the reliability of the Bible later, but we don't even need to get into that to dispose of this theory. We don't need to, because this is a non-issue for expert scholars of antiquity. Anyone who denies the existence of Jesus, the man, simply isn't being honest with what the facts show.

To hammer this point home, we reference Bart Ehrman. Bart is a world-class New Testament scholar who has authored six New York Times bestsellers. He is currently a Distinguished Professor of Religious Studies at the University of North Carolina at Chapel Hill. We reference Bart specifically because he is *not a Christian*. He is an "agnostic with atheist leanings." He has no desire to promote Christianity, but he is a historian to whom "evidence and the past matters." His position is that atheists who promote the idea that Jesus never existed are doing themselves a disservice because "frankly, it makes you look foolish to the outside world. It's not even an issue for scholars of antiquity. It's abundantly attested in early sources." He knows of no accredited university specialists in the field of religion, no matter how liberal or atheist, that teach that Jesus never lived.[4]

To put a bow on this, I'll reference my favorite personal finance expert, Dave Ramsey. Dave has been hosting a three-hour call-in fi-

---

4. Bart Ehrman, *"Did Jesus Exist?"*, YouTube video.

nancial advice talk show since 1992. Eighteen million listeners tune into the show per week. Dave is also the author of the New York Times Best Seller "Total Money Makeover."

Dave teaches that "taking financial advice from broke people is like taking dieting advice from overweight and out-of-shape people. In other words, it's dumb." Now, think about where you go to get your advice about God. Someone who believes Jesus, the man, is "about as real as the tooth fairy" is *spiritually broke*. We pray that God would open their eyes to see the truth, but in the meantime, they're certainly not where you'd want to go for spiritual counsel.

It's undeniable that Jesus, the man, existed. But was he just a human like you and me, or is He something more? In other words:

Dead or God?

Now that we've added responses #1-10 from our Newsweek list into *Fib*, we turn our attention to #11-20. Some of these responses shed Jesus in a favorable light, and others portray Him negatively. Some use flowery language to discuss an individual trait, or His ethnicity, or His imagined political affiliations, etc. Some paint Him as a teacher, and others, as a fool. The responses seem to run the gamut, but the reality is that they all essentially say the same thing: he was just a guy. Whether he was moral, bipolar, enlightened, compassionate, schizophrenic, or otherwise, these responses say he was just a guy. Notice that in these responses, He's generally referred to in the past tense, as if He is dead. Therefore, we can categorize responses #11-20 as *Dead*.

So, if #1-10 are *Fib* and #11-20 are *Dead*, where can we find some good examples of God? The Bible, of course! The Bible teaches that Jesus is literally God in the flesh. It teaches that He is fully God and fully human. Therefore, a Christian doesn't need to "recreate the wheel" when defining Jesus. We simply refer to the Bible. There is no shortage of titles we can reference that would fall within our God category. To name a few:

- I am

- The Messiah

- The Son of God

- The Son of Man

- The Way, The Truth, and The Life

- The King of Kings

- The Light of the World

- The Resurrection and The Life

- The Good Shepherd

- The Savior of the Whole World

Do you see the difference here?

Biblical titles for Jesus convey who He is; Dead responses attempt to tell us what kind of guy he was.

This leads us to a crossroads. We know that Jesus, the man, existed, and we know the Bible teaches that He's God. But, to get to the truth, we must examine the very structural integrity of the Christian faith – *the resurrection*.

Let's go.

***

Chapter 3

DECISION POINT

y five-year-old daughter is learning her basic addition and
subtraction in school. God help her because I barely made it
through pre-algebra, but that's beside the point. The point is that she's
learning objectively true things. For instance, $2 + 2 = 4$. That's true for
everybody, everywhere, always. Even if no one were on the planet, two
apple trees + two pear trees would still equal four trees in total.

If she has a test, my wife and I can work with her and make sure she
knows that $2 + 2 = 4$. That's the right thing to do, and we should do
it. But that's not what makes it true. It's true on its own. So, whether
we teach her correctly, teach her the wrong thing, or don't teach her
at all, $2 + 2$ still equals 4.

Now let's apply this logic to the topic at hand. Some people have
faith in God because their parents brought them up that way. That's a
beautiful thing, but is it a firm foundation? Let's check it against what
the Bible teaches:

*"And if you didn't grow up going to church with your
parents, your faith is futile; you are still in your sins."*

That doesn't sound quite right. Let's try again. What if my daughter feels deeply in her heart that 2 + 2 = 4? Based on her personal experiences and feelings, she just knows 2 + 2 = 4. Again, I say to you, that's not what makes it true. She can feel deeply that 2 + 2 = 4 or 24 or 2,024. That has no bearing on the truth of it.

Likewise, some people have faith in God because they've tried it, and it changed their lives for the better. That's a beautiful thing, but is that a firm foundation? Let's check it:

*"And if you haven't had a personal experience with God
that changed your life for the better, your faith is futile;
you are still in your sins."*

For anyone familiar with the passage, you know we're still not there. I submit to you that if our faith is based solely on what our parents teach us or based solely on our feelings, we're not on a solid footing. Every parent is a person, and therefore, has been wrong about things in their lives. And as for feelings, we know we can't trust them. I've felt things deep in my heart before that turned out to be flat wrong. Even the dictionary tells us this. "Feeling" is defined as "a belief, especially a vague or irrational one." Personal testimony is a powerful tool, and we're right to use it, but that's not in and of itself what makes Christianity true. There are people who have personal testimonies about all sorts of religions, but it doesn't make those religions true.

The bottom line is that I don't believe we can rightfully use our upbringing or our feelings as the ultimate decision point for Fib, Dead, or God.

Those things are subjective. Let's examine what the Bible actually teaches us:

> *"And **if Christ has not been raised**, your faith is futile; you are still in your sins."* [1]

Now we're talking! Talk about laying your cards down on the table. This verse exemplifies something highly unique about Christianity. Unlike other religions, Christianity can be tested because it hinges upon an actual event in history — the resurrection. **The resurrection is the ultimate decision point for *Fib, Dead, or God*.** If the resurrection is true, Jesus is *God*. If the resurrection is false, Jesus is *Dead*. And *Fibbers*... you've already been voted off the island. Sorry, not sorry.

I realize this approach clashes with modern cultural trends that emphasize the idea of "living your truth." But seeing as we're talking about the most crucial question in history here, we're going to focus on finding ***the truth***. Very simply: either this event happened, or it didn't. You can choose to believe it or not, and you can feel however you'd like to about it, but those things have no bearing on whether the event actually occurred. Thankfully, we have a tried-and-true method to investigate this historical event. Let's explore it.

---

1. 1 Cor 15:14

***

Chapter 4

F.A.C.T.S.

To investigate the resurrection and get at the truth, we will utilize the *minimal facts approach.*[1] This methodology was developed by American historian and New Testament Scholar, Dr. Gary Habermas. Dr. Habermas has dedicated his professional life to examining the resurrection of Jesus and is a world-class authority in this discipline. His minimal facts approach uses only evidence considered virtually undeniable, *even to skeptics.* To qualify:

- The facts must be confirmed by several strong and independent arguments.

- The facts must be recognized as historical by the vast majority of scholars who specialize in a relevant field of study. These are facts that liberal and even atheist scholars accept.

---

1. Gary Habermas, *The Case for the Resurrection of Jesus* (Grand Rapids, Michigan: Kregel Publications, 2004), 43.

These facts come not only from the Bible but also from numerous non-biblical sources. Some are even sources hostile to Christianity. Based on these undeniable historical facts, I submit to you this declaration of truth:

I choose to believe Jesus rose from the dead due to F.A.C.T.S.

By F.A.C.T.S., I mean: *Final breath, Appearances, Change, Taught, Skeptics* ©[2]. Say it with me five times, friend.

- Final breath, Appearances, Change, Taught, Skeptics.

- Final breath, Appearances, Change, Taught, Skeptics.

- Final breath, Appearances, Change, Taught, Skeptics.

- Final breath, Appearances, Change, Taught, Skeptics.

- Final breath, Appearances, Change, Taught, Skeptics.

With a bit of practice, it'll start to roll right off of your tongue. I designed it to be easy to remember. So, let's break it down.

F: *Final breath.* Jesus died by crucifixion. Undeniable fact.

A: *Appearances.* Very soon afterward, His followers had real experiences that they believed were appearances of the risen Jesus. Undeniable fact.

---

2. Copyright 2021 by James Finke; Living Sacrifice Books, LLC.

C: *Change*. As in radical change. His followers' lives were transformed due to these appearances, to the point that they were willing to die specifically for their faith in the resurrection. Undeniable fact.

T: *Taught*. These things were taught very early, soon after the crucifixion. They proclaimed Jesus as the Messiah, the Son of the Living God. Undeniable fact.

S: *Skeptics*. Some of the most unlikely people were converted after experiences that they believed were appearances from the risen Jesus. This includes James, the unbelieving brother of Jesus, and Saul of Tarsus (Paul), a persecutor specifically chosen to round up and arrest Christians. Undeniable fact.

Take a minute to digest these facts. Please keep in mind that they are accepted as historical even by atheist scholars who specialize in this discipline. When combined, we can walk through the fact pattern and take it to its logical conclusion:

Jesus died on the cross. Shortly after, His followers had real experiences they believed were appearances from the risen Jesus. Their lives changed radically. They went from hiding and being scared for their lives, to boldly preaching that Jesus is God in the flesh. They taught this despite that they had every human reason not to. Becoming Christians and teaching the resurrection caused them to be ostracized, tortured, and for most of Jesus' closest followers, brutally killed. Some of the most unlikely people were converted, following experiences that they believed were appearances from the risen Jesus. That includes James, the brother of Jesus, who thought Jesus was insane before his crucifixion. Also, Paul, who was a fervent persecutor of early Christians. Both became Christians and were ultimately martyred for preaching that Jesus is God.

Deep breath.

As miraculous as it is, I submit that the only reasonable conclusion we can draw from this fact pattern is, <u>Jesus was telling the truth.</u>

Recall what He said to the Jews before his crucifixion:

> *"The Jews then responded to him, 'What sign can you show us to prove your authority to do all this?' Jesus answered them, 'Destroy this temple, and I will raise it again in three days.' They replied, 'It has taken forty-six years to build this temple, and you are going to raise it in three days?'* **But the temple he had spoken of was his body.**" [3]

Skeptics have no good answer for F.A.C.T.S. because there is no good answer outside of the truth. But it's not for lack of trying. Over the centuries, various "alternative theories" have been proposed, all of which have been debunked. For example:

• *Conspiracy Theory* - This one essentially says the disciples stole the body and made up the resurrection story. Really? The Bible tells us that Jesus appeared to over 500 followers at the same time. Am I to believe that over 500 followers were in on a lie and kept it a secret

---

3. John 2:18-21, emphasis mine.

for more than 60 years? All the while they were scattered around the Roman Empire being persecuted, tortured, and killed? Former Cold-Case homicide detective, J. Warner Wallace, is an expert in this arena and shows that this makes for a terrible conspiracy theory by every measure. Liars make poor martyrs. If this topic interests you further, I'd recommend his book, Cold-Case Christianity.

• *Swoon Theory* - This one says that Jesus did not actually die on the cross. Instead, He fainted and was placed in the tomb alive. This theory is even espoused in the Koran, written 700 years after the crucifixion.[4] This theory has been destroyed, first and foremost by medical doctors. In "The Case for Christ," Lee Strobel interviews Dr. Alexander Metherell, M.D., Ph.D. He is an expert on the historical, archaeological, and medical data concerning the death of Jesus. He describes (in brutal detail) the beating, flogging, crucifixion, and finally, the spear in the side that Jesus received. His bottom-line is that the idea that Jesus survived the cross is "Impossible. It's a fanciful theory without any possible basis in fact." So, this theory essentially says Jesus survived the cross despite what the facts show. In his near-dead state, He somehow rolled away the stone blocking the tomb without Roman guards noticing. Also, would the disciples immediately begin worshipping Him as God if He were half-dead and recovering? This theory makes no sense.

• *Group Hallucinations* - This one says that the many people who saw Jesus in His resurrected body were hallucinating. We know this

---

4. Gary Habermas, "Reinterpretations of the Historical Jesus," YouTube Video.

isn't true based on what science has taught us about hallucinations. Dr. Michael Licona, a professor of theology, sums it up: "Hallucinations are like dreams. They are private occurrences... You could not share a hallucination you were having with someone any more than you could wake up your spouse in the middle of the night and ask him or her to join you in a dream you were having."[5] The idea of 500 people having the same hallucination and changing their beliefs because of it is nonsensical.

I say to you again: **I choose to believe Jesus rose from the dead due to F.A.C.T.S**. But what if you're not sure? There's something you should know...

***

---

5. *Josh McDowell Ministries*

Chapter 5

ROOM-TEMPERATURE FAITH

Americans drink about 400 *million* cups of coffee every day. We drink more coffee than soda, tea, and juice combined.[1] It's serious business. For many, coffee is an integral part of their daily routine, so much so that over half of all coffee consumers would rather skip a shower in the morning than skip their coffee.[2] I must say, these stats are very comforting to me. It's nice to know that I'm not the only lunatic who sometimes goes to bed already looking forward to the next morning's black coffee.

---

1. Marketwatch.com

2. Huffpost - America's Coffee Obsession.

In terms of variety, there seems to be as many ways to take your coffee as there are coffee drinkers — hot, iced, cold-brew, nitro, cappuccinos, lattes, frappes, espressos, flavors, sweeteners, different types of beans... it's endless. Some people get their fix from local coffee shops, while others brew their own at home. Personally, I make most of my coffee at home. With a coffeemaker right in my office, it's both convenient and budget-friendly. I also think the coffee tastes better from a mug than in a paper to-go cup.

The only problem is the temperature. As good as the coffee is, when brewed hot and fresh, it goes downhill in a hurry as it sits in the mug and cools off. To combat this, I've worked out a system where I brew the coffee into a special covered thermos that keeps it molten hot. I can then pour it into my mug in small increments and enjoy it at my preferred temperature.

There's iced coffee on the other end of the spectrum, which is also delicious, especially when the weather is sunny and hot. Here in New England, many welcome the change in season from Winter to Spring with a change in coffee; from hot to iced.

In summary: It's great when it's hot, it's great when it's iced, but it's lousy when it's lukewarm.

Do you realize that our faith in the living God is also lousy when it's lukewarm? I call this a *Room Temperature Faith*.

Someone with a Room Temperature Faith is not "on fire" for God, nor are they a diehard atheist. Instead, they're undecided, uncommitted, and generally indifferent. Rather than follow the F.A.C.T.S. to their only logical conclusion, these people choose to draw *no conclusion at all*. They remain on the fence, which is a treacherous place to be.

Pastor Todd White tells a true story about an atheist who has a dream. The man dreams he's in a vast field, and there's a fence that goes right up the middle. On one side is Jesus with a group of people, and on the other side, there's the devil with another group of people. The guy stands up on the fence, and all of a sudden, he's by himself. The devil comes back into the picture and says, "There you are; I was looking for you." And the man said, "Hey, I didn't choose Jesus, but I sure didn't choose you." And the devil said, "**Sure, you did. I own the fence**." The man woke up a Christian.[3]

What I'm telling you is, "**I'm not sure**" means you're rejecting **Jesus as *God***. Paradoxically, when you avoid deciding, you are actually choosing to be an unbeliever. Jesus said, "*Whoever is not with me is against me, and whoever does not gather with me scatters.*" [4] In other words, there is no middle ground.

***

---

3. Todd White, "My Testimony," YouTube video.

4. Matthew 12:30

PART 1 REVIEW

L et's recap what we know:

1. Many of us spend so much time and energy focusing on secondary issues that we miss the very foundation of the Christian faith: *If Jesus rose from the dead, Christianity is true.*

2. Rather than fruitlessly playing Spiritual Whac-A-Mole, we can get to the heart of the matter, using *Fib, Dead, or God.*

3. The ultimate decision point for *Fib, Dead, or God* is not based on something subjective, like our upbringing or our feelings. Rather, it is objective truth based on the actual historical event of the resurrection of Jesus.

4. Final Breath, Appearances, Change, Taught, Skeptics are undeniable facts that are accepted even by atheist specialist scholars.

5. "Undecided" is a decision to be an unbeliever.

It's time we pull back the curtain on this question we're seeking to answer:

> *"When Jesus came into the region of Caesarea Phillipi,*
> *He asked His disciples, 'Who do men say that I, the*
> *Son of Man, am?' So, they said, 'Some say John the*
> *Baptist, some, Elijah, and others, Jeremiah or one of the*

*prophets." He said to them, 'But who do **you** say that I am?'*

"Simon Peter answered and said, '**You are the Christ, the Son of the living God**.' Jesus answered and said to him, 'Blessed are you, Simon son of Jonah, for flesh and blood has not revealed this to you, but My Father who is in heaven."* [1]

Bottom Line #1: Jesus is the Son of God. The resurrection is the structural integrity of our faith.

Want the F.A.C.T.S. at your fingertips? We've got you covered. Click here for your copy of the *Fib, Dead, or God?* **F.A.C.T.S. Sheet**. It's printable and shareable.

***

---

1. Matthew 16:13-17

PART 2: THE BLUEPRINT OF OUR FAITH

Chapter 6

THE CHIEF CORNERSTONE

PART 2 - THE BLUEPRINT OF OUR FAITH

J esus Christ rose from the dead, closing the case that He is who he said He is – the Son of God. With sufficient evidence readily available, how is it that some people continue to reject Him, casting Him as a *Fib* or *Dead*? The answer is quite literally as old as humanity itself –

People want to be their own god.

To see how deep the roots of this problem go, let's consider this passage from the creation account in the book of Genesis. God tells Adam and Eve they can eat from any tree in the Garden of Eden, other than the tree of knowledge of good and evil. If they eat from that tree, they will certainly die. That's a straightforward instruction if I've ever heard one. Now, let's pick it up from Genesis 3:1.

> *Now the serpent (Satan) was more crafty than any of the wild animals the Lord God had made. He said to the woman, "Did God really say, 'you must not eat from any tree in the garden'?" The woman said to the serpent, "We may eat fruit from the trees in the garden, but God did say, 'You must not eat fruit from the tree that is in the middle of the garden, and you must not touch it, or you will die.'" "You will not certainly die," the serpent said to the woman. "For God knows that when you eat from it, your eyes will be opened, and **you will be like God**, knowing good and evil."* [1]

You know how the story goes. Adam and Eve succumbed to the temptation, disobeyed God, and ate the fruit. It's no big deal; all they did was cause *the fall* of the entire human race! *The fall* is why you don't know a single person who has lived a perfectly sin-free life. Since the fall, every one of us has been born with a sinful nature, living in rebellion against our Creator, all because of that age-old seduction to be our own god.

This temptation is illustrated famously by Tony Montana, the cocaine kingpin in the classic movie *Scarface*, as he assesses his drug empire. "Who do you think put this thing together? Me! That's who. Who do I trust? Me!" In the end, it didn't work out too great for Tony,

---

1. Genesis 3:1-5

nor will it work out well for anyone who rejects Jesus so they can try to be their own god. But, unfortunately, this temptation has its marks all over our culture. Any of this sound familiar to you?

> *"In the end, the only person you can truly rely on is yourself. In the end, you're all you've got. You have everything you need inside of you. The entire universe lies inside of you. The power comes from within. You can do anything you set your mind to. You are entirely up to you. No one can stop you. You just need to live your truth. Do what you want, who am I to judge? Your body, your choice. It's all about self-confidence. A lion doesn't concern himself with the opinions of sheep."*

Of course, this approach to living runs in diametric opposition to what Jesus taught, which was *radical surrender*:

> *"Then Jesus said to his disciples, 'If you truly want to follow me, you should at once completely reject and dis-own your own life. And you must be willing to share my cross and experience it as your own, as you **continually surrender to my ways**. For if you choose self-sacrifice and lose your lives for my glory, you will continually discover true life. But if you choose to keep your lives for yourselves, you will forfeit what you try to keep. For even if you were to gain all the wealth and power of the world - at the cost of your own life - what good would that be? And what could be more valuable to you than your own soul?'"* [2]

---

2. Matthew 16:24-26

Is it any wonder that there are still unbelievers out there? It's not because of a lack of evidence; it's because of a lack of obedience.

We naturally want to design our lives around our own desires, but following Jesus requires continually surrendering to His ways. In other words, we must accept that Jesus is the *Chief Cornerstone*. Please allow me to explain because you may not be familiar with that term unless you happen to be an architect. A cornerstone is traditionally the first stone laid for a structure, with all other stones laid in reference to it.[3] We find this concept used throughout the Bible, pointing to the one true cornerstone. Indeed, hundreds of years before the birth of Jesus, major Jewish prophets foretold of this cornerstone that was to come from God.

> *"So, this is what the Sovereign Lord says: 'See, I lay a stone in Zion, a tested stone, a precious **cornerstone** for a sure foundation; the one who relies on it will never be stricken with panic."* [4]

This tells us that since Jesus is the Chief Cornerstone, every other "stone" of our life is supposed to be laid

---

3. Newstudioarchitecture.com

4. Isaiah 28:16

in reference to Him. It's this life design that makes for a firm foundation.

For anyone who doubts whether Jesus holds this position, I want you to know that The Office of the Chief Cornerstone is an equal opportunity employer. Since the foundation of the whole world relies on this position, the office just needs to verify your credentials. You are strongly encouraged to apply, so long as you predict and then prove that you would suffer, be killed, and be raised to life again three days later.

Listen, it comes down to a matter of trust. We're not talking about blind faith because God has given us sufficient evidence. The Bible tells us that *"those who know His name, put their trust in Him."* [5]

We know His name. His name is the Son of God. He's not a *Fib,* and He's not *Dead.* Jesus is the Chief Cornerstone, and His resurrection is the structural integrity of our faith.

As we move forward, we'll dig deeper into this issue. Just as man's desire to be god has roots back to the dawn of humanity, so is Satan's tactic for exploiting that desire. It's time we expose it, so we will be prepared when we inevitably encounter it. Let's go.

***

---

5. Psalms 9:10

Chapter 7

SPIRITUAL TAPE MEASURE

I remember exactly where I was when I first heard that a plane had hit the World Trade Center on September 11, 2001. For anyone that was old enough at the time, it's one of those moments that get etched into your memory forever. I was in class, AP History, with Mr. Morgan. When we first heard it, the other kids and I thought it was a joke. We pictured some single-occupancy prop plane making a wrong turn and clipping a wing on a building. In retrospect, that too would have been tragic and should not have been joked about, but that's what you get as a first reaction from a group of knuckleheaded 16-year-olds. At that time, I was only a couple of years away from entering the phase of my life that I would like to refer to as "peak idiot."

In any sense, we all know that 9/11 was one of the most infamous and tragic days in American history. It caused changes in our world that remain evident today, over 20 years later. For example, the Transportation Security Administration (TSA) was formed within months of the attack, and the U.S. has subsequently spent over $100 billion to secure airports and airplanes. [1] Among other changes, cockpits are now sealed off and inaccessible during flights, armed air marshals patrol flights undercover, and the entire airport screening process has been overhauled. Naturally, these things have been done to learn from the tragedy and prevent a similar attack from ever occurring again.

As the saying made famous by Winston Churchill goes, "Those who fail to learn from history are doomed to repeat it." So, what can we learn from *The Fall*? Let's go back to the text to identify the crime:

> *Now, the serpent (Satan) was more crafty than any of the wild animals the Lord God had made. He said to the woman, "**Did God really say**, 'you must not eat from any tree in the garden'?" The woman said to the serpent, "We may eat fruit from the trees in the garden, but God did say, 'You must not eat fruit from the tree that is in the middle of the garden, and you must not touch it, or you will die.'" "You will not certainly die," the serpent said to the woman. "For God knows that when you eat from it, your eyes will be opened, and **you will be like God**, knowing good and evil."* [2]

Do you see it? It's as plain as day.

---

1. cntraveler.com

2. Genesis 3:1-5

Satan questioned the authority of the Word of God to exploit our desire to be our own god.

Authority Questioned	To Exploit our Desire
"Did God *really* say…?"	"Your eyes will be opened, and you will be like God."

This was no accident. It should be instructive to us that Satan attacked humanity by questioning God's Word. Just as the 9/11 terrorists targeted New York City and Washington DC to inflict the maximum possible damage, Satan targeted God's Word to do likewise. That is evidence of just how important God's word is to our faith.

Now, you may be wondering, "What does this have to do with us today? God is not speaking to me in the Garden of Eden." **It's about the Bible, friend!** God left us His inspired, authoritative Word in the form of the Bible, and it's an invaluable tool for us. **Satan targeted the Bible because it's our spiritual tape measure.**

If you've ever observed a builder at work, they almost certainly have a tape measure nearby. This tool is so vital that it generally always stays on their person, clipped to their belt or pocket. Why is that? It's the old adage of "measure twice, cut once." Builders *constantly measure*, in order to get their bearings to make decisions.

So, it is with our faith. We have the design: Jesus is the Chief Cornerstone, and every other "stone of our life" is supposed to be laid in reference to Him. To do that, we should constantly be measuring by the Word of God.

Is it any question why the Word of God has been under attack since the dawn of humanity? If we're going to learn from history, we must choose God's word over our desire to be in control and be our own god.

But how can we be sure this 2,000+ year old book still applies to our lives today?

***

Chapter 8

IT IS WRITTEN

"I'm just not sure. The Bible has been translated so many times, we don't have the originals, and the ones we do have are er-ror-ridden; the Bible has been altered over time, humans wrote it, so it's just a human book with what they believed about God, it's scientifically inaccurate, it's no longer applicable to modern living, etc."

By now, I trust you recognize Spiritual Whac-A-Mole when you see it. The list of objections to the Bible is endless because it's by far the most scrutinized book in history. Skeptics have been trying to disprove and discredit the Bible for thousands of years. They couldn't do it then, they can't do it now, and they'll never be able to do it. Meanwhile, billions of people continue to stake their eternal life on what the Bible says.

The beautiful thing is: *Fib, Dead, or God* **still applies!** Just as with any other issue surrounding our faith, our starting point is the resurrection. After that, we simply take the next logical step along the path:

I choose to believe Jesus rose from the dead due to
F.A.C.T.S. Therefore, Jesus proved He is who He said
He is – the Son of God. Since Jesus is the Son of God,
my view of the Bible is based on what <u>He</u> taught
about it.

So, what did Jesus teach about the Bible? [1]

- **It's timeless** - Today, many believe that the Bible no longer applies to modern living. But Jesus said, "It is easier for heaven and earth to pass away than for one stroke of a letter of God's Law to fail and become void."

- **It's inerrant** - When a group of religious Jews posed a hypothetical situation to call the Bible into question, Jesus told them, "You are mistaken, not knowing the Scriptures, nor the power of God." In other words, God's Word can't be wrong, so, that leaves *you* to be in error for not knowing it.

- **It's historically accurate** - Skeptics scoff at many Biblical events, writing them off as myths. But Jesus affirmed things like the Great Flood, Moses Lifting the Snake, and Sodom and Gomorrah as actual historical events. "And as it was in the days of Noah, so it will be also in the days of the Son of Man: They ate, they drank, they married wives, they were

---

1. Alisa Childers, "What Did Jesus Say About the Bible?" YouTube video.

given in marriage, until the day that Noah entered the ark, and the flood came and destroyed them all."

- **It's inspired by the Holy Spirit** - Understandably, many people struggle with the idea that the Bible is "God-breathed." They consider it to be a human book because humans wrote it down. But that's not what Jesus taught. He affirmed that the Holy Spirit inspired the writing of scripture. He described that David wrote Old Testament Psalms "in the Spirit." He promised His Apostles that the Holy Spirit would be sent to superintend their writings, which we now know as the New Testament. "But the Helper, the Holy Spirit, whom the Father will send in My name, He will teach you all things, and *bring to your remembrance all things that I said to you.*"

The bottom line is: Jesus taught that the Bible is the authoritative Word of God.

Jesus quotes from the Old Testament, saying, "*For <u>God commanded</u>*" or "*Have you not read what was spoken to you <u>by God</u>?*" He also promises us the New Testament, saying, "*Heaven and earth will pass away, but My words will by no means pass away.*"

For those of you keeping score at home:

Joe Skeptic	Jesus Christ, the Son of God
The Bible no longer applies to modern living.	Heaven and earth will pass away, but My words will by no means pass away.
There are errors in the Bible.	*You are mistaken* for not knowing the scriptures.
The Bible is a bunch of myths and fairytales.	It's easier for heaven and earth to pass away than for one tiny mark of the law to fail and become void.
It's a human book.	Have you not read what was *spoken to you by God*?
I need to live my truth.	The Bible is the truth, the authoritative Word of God.

Honestly... who's judgment would you trust?

We're back to our principle of not getting financial advice from your broke friend or dieting advice from your out-of-shape relative. When it comes to the Word of God, I'll take my cues from what the Son of God has to say about it. As Pastor Andy Stanley put it, "My high school science teacher once told me that much of Genesis is false. But since my high school science teacher did not prove he was God by rising from the dead, I'm going to believe Jesus instead."

Jesus not only taught that the Bible is the Word of God, but He also modeled for us how to use it. When the devil tried to tempt Jesus to sin, He overcame it by using the scriptures.

"Then Jesus was led by the Spirit into the wilderness to be tempted by the devil. After fasting forty days and forty nights, He was hungry. The tempter (Satan) came to Him and said, 'If you are the Son of God, tell these stones to become bread.'[2]

Jesus disposes of the temptation by measuring it against what the Bible says. When Jesus says, *"it is written,"* it means He is quoting Old Testament scripture. *"It is written,"* is the equivalent of Him saying, "God says."

Jesus answered, 'It is written (God says): Man shall not live on bread alone, but on every word that comes from the mouth of God.'[3]

In other words, what you're tempting Me to do doesn't line up with the Word of God, so I know it's wrong. So next, Satan tries to twist the Bible to get Jesus to sin:

Then the devil took Him to the holy city and had him stand on the highest point of the temple. "If you are the Son of God," he said, "throw yourself down. For it is written, 'He will command his angels concerning you,

---

2. Matthew 4:1-3

3. Matthew 4:4, Jesus quoting Deut. 8:3

and they will lift you up in their hands, so that you will
not strike your foot against a stone.'" [4]

We should not be surprised when unbelievers attempt to twist
scripture to use it against Christians. It happened to Jesus himself.
When we consider the breadth of the Bible, it's easy to see how fraud-
ulent attempts can be made using as little as a single verse. The Bible
is a collection of 66 volumes written by over 40 authors from different
walks of life and located on three continents. It touches on hundreds
of subjects and was written in three different languages over a period
of 1,500 years. Yet, astonishingly, these books come together to tell one
story of Jesus saving the world.

As Greg Koukl explains in his book *Stand to Reason*, "If there was
one bit of wisdom, one rule of thumb, one single skill I could impart,
one useful tip I could leave that would serve you well the rest of your
life, what would it be? What is the single most important practice skill
I've ever learned as a Christian? Here it is: Never read a Bible verse.
That's right, never read a Bible verse. Instead, always read a paragraph
at least."

Greg is hammering home the point that if there is an error, it's
not in the scripture; it's in our understanding of that scripture. The
scripture is the standard of truth, which is why Jesus again disposes of
the temptation by measuring it against what the Bible says:

---

4. Matthew 4:5-6.

Jesus answered him, "It is also written: 'Do not put the Lord your God to the test.'" [5]

Satan gives it one last try:

"Again, the devil took him to a very high mountain and showed Him all the kingdoms of the world and their splendor. 'All this I will give to you,' he said, 'if you will bow down and worship me.'" [6]

Sound familiar? Temptations always come back to enjoying the short-term pleasures of the world. But Jesus finally gets rid of the devil using the Word of God. He rejects a worldly temptation for a heavenly alternative.

Jesus said to him, "Away from me, Satan! For it is written: 'Worship the Lord your God, and serve Him only.'" [7]

This exchange is a rock-solid example for us as to the power of the Word of God. When temptations arise, our job is to use our spiritual tape measure (the Bible!) to determine if it lines up with the Chief Cornerstone. If it's not aligned with Jesus, that "stone" needs

---

5. Matthew 4:7, Jesus quoting Deut. 6:16.

6. Matthew 4:8-9 NIV.

7. Matthew 4: 8-10, Jesus quoting Deut. 6:13

to change, or you need to remove it from your life. Let's lay our next stone:

Since Jesus is the Son of God, my view of the Bible is based on what <u>He</u> taught about it. He taught that the Bible is the authoritative Word of God. Therefore, my #1 priority is to live in agreement with what it says.

***

PART 2 REVIEW

L et's recap what we know:

1. People want to be their own god, but since Jesus is the Chief Cornerstone, every other "stone" of our life is supposed to be laid in reference to <u>Him.</u>

2. Since the dawn of humanity, Satan has questioned the authority of the word of God to exploit our desire to be god.

3. Because Jesus is the Son of God, my view of the Bible is shaped by what <u>He</u> taught about it.

4. Jesus taught that the Bible is the authoritative Word of God.

5. The Bible is our spiritual tape measure.

"Whoever believes in the Son accepts His testimony. Whoever does not believe God has made Him out to be a liar, because they have not believed the testimony God has given about his Son. And this is the testimony: God has given us eternal life, and this life is in His son. Whoever has the Son has life; whoever does not have the Son of God does not have life."[1]

---

1. 1 John 5:10-12

Bottom line #2: The Bible is the Word of God. It is our spiritual tape measure; a tool to build our lives in alignment with the Chief Cornerstone, Jesus.

***

PART 3: THE GOOD NEWS OF OUR FAITH

Chapter 9

HOUSTON, WE HAVE A PROBLEM

PART 3 - THE GOOD NEWS OF OUR FAITH

The Apollo 13 spacecraft was launched from Kennedy Space Center on April 11th, 1970. The mission to land on the moon was aborted after an oxygen tank in the service module failed, two days into the operation. The world watched with bated breath as the spacecraft miraculously returned safely to Earth on April 17th.

Perhaps the most enduring symbol of the Apollo 13 mission is the phrase, "Houston, we have a problem." This is a quotation from the radio communications between Astronaut Jack Swigert and the NASA Mission Control Center (Houston). Swigert was communicating the discovery of the explosion that crippled their spacecraft. The blast caused a loss of all oxygen stores and a loss of water, electrical power, and propulsion system use. All of this occurred while the spacecraft was nearly 200,000 miles away from Earth.[1] It's difficult to imagine circumstances more dire. *And yet, the Bible teaches that we all have an infinitely more crucial problem.* That's not a hyperbole. The authoritative Word of God identifies a problem that continues to impact every person in history and has *eternal* consequences. It is precisely the issue Jesus came to settle.

The problem is sin. Consider its breadth: The Bible has 1,189 chapters in it. Only four involve a world devoid of sin — the first two and the last two.[2] The middle 1,185 sin-filled chapters span from the creation of the universe to its destruction. So, it's an all-encompassing problem. That said, allow me to personalize it to help bring into focus how it impacts us individually:

- God is perfectly Holy, so, wrongdoing cannot exist in His presence. *"Your eyes are too pure to look on evil; you cannot tolerate wrongdoing."*[3]

- I am basically a walking "wrongdoing." *"For all have sinned and fall short of the glory of God."*[4]

---

1. Nasa.gov

2. John MacArthur, "Winning the Battle Against Sin – Part 1," YouTube video.

3. Habakkuk 1:13

4. Romans 3:23

Houston, we have a problem.

And just in case I'm too subtle when I say "we," I'm saying that **you**, friend, are included in this problem.

The Authoritative Word of God says sin is the single most crucial problem in your life and mine.

How can I say that without even knowing you? It's because the Bible tells us that **all** people have sinned and fall short of the glory of God. *"If we say that we have no sin, we deceive ourselves, and the truth is not in us."* [5]

The first two chapters of the Bible describe the creation of the universe and humanity. God created humans, beginning with Adam and Eve, to live in harmony and fellowship with Him forever. Immediately following Creation, we read in Chapter 3 about the "Fall of Man" (*The Fall*). Adam and Eve questioned the Word of God and disobeyed Him. It was here that we first encountered the ultimate and direct consequence of sin; *sin causes separation from God.* God banished Adam and Eve from the Garden of Eden.

Now, as bad as living an Earthly life separated from our Creator God is, what's worse is that unless something changes, we'll remain separated from Him during our afterlife... for eternity. That doesn't sound pleasant. In fact, we have a word for an afterlife lived apart from

---

5. 1 John 1:8

God – it's called hell. That's why the Bible teaches us that *"the wages of sin is death."*[6] It describes an eternal separation from God as a result of our sin.

When most people think about hell, they think it is a place reserved for sinners other than ourselves; i.e., people who are "worse" than us. We think of people like Adolf Hitler. Hitler was responsible for the genocide of about six million Jews and the killing of over *50 million* people overall. That's an unfathomable level of evil.

Would it seem right to you if, after unapologetically sinning until he committed suicide, God rewarded Hitler and welcomed him into heaven with open arms? Of course not. And the reason why that idea is so repugnant to us is that we are made in the image of God. God is perfectly just, so we are created with a deep yearning for fairness and justice. That can even be seen in our children. Virtually as soon as they can communicate, they begin to let us know what they believe is "not fair."

Because we yearn for justice, deep down, we know that we must be punished for our sins. Anything less would be unjust, and our perfectly Holy God is perfectly just. The Word of God affirms that the sinner must get what they deserve. *"Do not be deceived: God cannot be mocked. A man reaps what he sows."*[7] So, if we plant sin during our earthly lives, we reap separation from God in our afterlives. It's that

---

6. Romans 6:23

7. Galatians 6:7

simple. Psalm 5:4 states it plainly: *"For You are not a God who takes pleasure in wickedness; No evil [person] dwells with You."*

Now, you may be thinking, *"Wicked? Evil? Isn't that kind of harsh? I know I'm not perfect, but I'm not so bad. I'm a good person compared to many others out there. So, how could a loving God let me go to hell for eternity instead of dwelling with Him in heaven?"*

The critical error in this viewpoint is that it attempts to replace God's standards with our standards. When our point of reference is other sinners, we may, by comparison, look like a "good person." Even a murderer may seem "good" if he's compared to Hitler. But is that really the standard we believe God uses for admittance to dwell with Him eternally in heaven?

That's like expecting to earn your acceptance into the most prestigious medical school in the world despite having a transcript full of D's. The student with all F's may be "worse," but would it really be the most prestigious medical school in the world if that were the standard for admittance? We'd better get out our spiritual tape measure to find God's criteria:

> *"This is the message which we have heard from Him and declare to you, that God is light and **in Him is no darkness at all.**"* [8]

---

8. 1 John 1:5

No darkness at all. None. In other words, God's standard is perfect Holiness because He is perfectly Holy. No sin can exist in His presence. There is an infinite gap between sin and our perfectly Holy God.

If that seems like an impossible standard to meet, it's because it is indeed an impossible standard to meet... *since The Fall*. The Fall introduced sin, and therefore, death to the world. All humans, as heirs of Adam and Eve, are born sinners *by nature*. Think about it. Even the most righteous people on Earth have some measure of darkness within them. The Word says as much, "*Therefore, just as sin entered the world through one man, and death through sin, and in this way, death came to all people, because **all** sinned.*" [9]

Even if you'd never read the Bible, it's evident that there isn't a single perfect person walking this earth. That's the beautiful thing about absolute truth. It's true regardless of how you feel about it or whether you believe it.

So, to summarize this dilemma: Absolutely no sin can exist in the presence of God, and absolutely every person on Earth has been infected with sin since *The Fall*. If we're going to be with God for eternity, it's either He needs to drop His standards, or we need to drop our sin. To lower His standards would mean that our God is no longer perfectly Holy, which is logically impossible.

Therefore, the only logical conclusion is, unless we can somehow remove ourselves from our sins, we

---

9. Romans 5:12

rightfully, justly, and necessarily will live our after-lives separated from God... in hell.

If you are not a Christian, the notion that we are all sinners and deserve to go to hell may be offensive to you. The truth is, I sincerely hope it is. Hear me out on this. Imagine you are out to dinner with a group of friends. A dear friend of yours is having a great time and enjoying several glasses of wine. You notice he is tipsy, and his speech is slurred. He continues drinking up until the end of the night when he pulls out his car keys to drive home. He's headed toward disaster. You can wish him well and just hope he makes it home safe, or you can take away his keys. The reality is, if you choose the latter, you're most likely going to offend him. He doesn't want to hear the truth that he is not fit to drive. It would be much easier to let him go his own way, but would it be more loving?

The same principle applies here. The Bible tells us that every one of us is headed for disaster. By ignoring this warning, we're just crossing our fingers and hoping our friend makes it home safe. It's the easy way out, and unfortunately, we see it all over our culture. Pastor Voddie Bauchum explains this sentiment masterfully, using what he calls the "11th commandment." Essentially, our culture disregards the first ten commandments in favor of the secular (godless) 11th commandment – thou shalt be nice.

It may seem "nice" to breeze over the parts of the Bible that make us uncomfortable, but it sure isn't loving. I'd rather lovingly offend you with the truth of God's Word than wish you well with a smile as you head toward disaster. Besides, this isn't the end of the story! We've identified this Biblical problem; let's go find a Biblical solution.

***

Chapter 10

REARRANGING DECK CHAIRS ON THE TITANIC

"I thought her unsinkable, and I based my opinion on the best expert advice available. I do not understand it." - Phillip Franklin, White Star Line Vice President, 1912. [1]

T he sinking of the RMS Titanic on April 15th, 1912, is perhaps the best-known shipwreck in history. The British passenger liner struck an iceberg and sunk on its maiden voyage from Southampton to New York. Over 1,500 died, ranging from some of

---

1. New York Times 04/16/1912.

the world's wealthiest people to impoverished immigrants seeking a new life in the U.S.

At the time, the Titanic was the largest moving human-made object in the world.[2] It had contemporary safety features like watertight compartments, and was generally believed to be unsinkable. As a result, the ship infamously had only enough lifeboats to carry about half of those on board, and the crew had not been adequately trained to launch an evacuation. Years earlier, the ship's captain was quoted as having said he "could not imagine any condition which would cause a ship to founder. Modern shipbuilding has gone beyond that."

The Titanic struck an iceberg just before midnight on April 14th while traveling at full speed through frigid waters south of Newfoundland. It's believed that the lookouts were unaware of the magnitude of the danger because the ice conditions in the North Atlantic were exceptionally harsh that year — the worst for any April in the previous fifty years. The collision caused the ship's hull plates to buckle inward and opened five of the sixteen watertight compartments to the sea; one more than the vessel could survive. When the ship's chief designer discovered that five of the watertight compartments were breached, he knew catastrophe was imminent, so, the ship was evacuated. Within three hours of impact, the Titanic had sunk. Less than 30% of those on board survived the night.

The sinking shocked the world and dominated the news cycle of the time. Unbelievably, the first film portraying the tragedy appeared just 29 days after the event, and it had an actual survivor as its star. Today,

---

2. Livescience.com

over 100 years later, the cultural impacts of the Titanic remain in the form of art, film, literature, memorials, replicas, museums, and more.

We even find its impacts within our language. For example, the phrase "rearranging deck chairs on the Titanic" is a well-known idiom to this day. It describes a well-meaning but futile action in the face of an imminent catastrophe.

Do you realize that when it comes to the problem of sin, our world is full of people who spend their lives rearranging deck chairs on the Titanic?

These efforts are the definition of futility, and they come in virtually every shape and size. They may be ceremonial, religious, moral, philanthropic, or otherwise. Essentially, people think, "If I can just perform these ceremonies, or pray enough, or do these sacraments, or meditate enough, or deny myself enough, or kill enough infidels, or become 'woke' enough, or achieve Zen, then I'll be right with God." The list goes on and on. One that is very popular in our culture today is the idea that "if I'm a 'good person,' then God owes me heaven, no matter my religion."

Here's the problem: There are no "good" people by God's standards. Remember, the Bible tells us that absolutely no sin can exist in God's presence. Has anything in your own life or anyone you've ever met given you evidence to believe a sin-free life is attainable? Of course not, and the Word says as much. *"As it is written and forever remains written, 'There is none righteous [none that meets God's standard], not even one.'"* [3]

We humans have been battling our sinful nature ever since The Fall. Even the Apostle Paul, the author of over half of the New Testament, fought this battle: *"For I do not understand my own actions [I am baffled and bewildered by them]. I do not practice what I want to do, but I am doing the very thing I hate [and yielding to my human nature, my worldliness, my sinful capacity] ... For the willingness [to do good] is present in me, but the doing of good is not."* [4] That was recorded nearly 2,000 years ago, yet, we can still identify with Paul's struggle today.

Since the Word of God establishes that not one of us meets God's standard, we're deceiving ourselves if we believe doing good deeds somehow cancels out the wrong things we've done in our lives. *For no person will be justified [freed of guilt and declared righteous] in His sight by [trying to do] the works of the Law.* [5] In fact, by God's standards, even our good deeds are an extension of our sinful nature. Our so-called "righteousness" is like filthy rags. *"For we all have become like one who is unclean, and all of our deeds of righteousness are like filthy rags; we all wither and decay like a leaf, and our wickedness, like the wind, takes us away toward destruction."* [6]

---

3. Romans 3:10

4. Romans 7:15, 18

5. Romans 3:20

6. Isaiah 64:6

The bottom line is this:

When it comes to the problem of sin, relying on yourself and what you can do is about as effective as you repairing the Titanic with a mop bucket and a roll of duct tape.

***

Chapter 11

SPIRITUAL SNELLEN TEST

The most crucial problem in your life and mine is something that we have absolutely no capacity to solve for ourselves. We can improve our behavior and perform good deeds all day long, but we can never live a sin-free life. This isn't new. It's been the human condition ever since *The Fall*. In other words, we can't save ourselves, so we need someone else to save us — a Savior. God has promised us just that!

By way of background, God used prophets to deliver messages to the nation of Israel for hundreds of years. At least, 60 major prophecies were recorded in the Old Testament of the Bible where God promises a Messiah (translated: Christ) who would save the world and sit on the throne forever. Take your time as you read through this one...

"He grew up like a small plant before the Lord. He was like a root growing in dry land. He had no special beau-

ty or form to make us notice him. There was nothing in his appearance to make us desire him.

He was hated and rejected by people. He had much pain and suffering. People would not even look at him. He was hated, and we didn't even notice him. But he took our suffering on him and felt our pain for us.

We saw his suffering. We thought God was punishing him. But he was pierced for the wrong things we did. He was crushed for the evil things we did. The punishment, which made us well, was given to him. And we are healed because of his wounds.

We all have wandered away like sheep. Each of us has gone his own way. But the Lord has put on him the punishment for all the evil we have done. He was beaten down and punished. But he didn't say a word. He was like a lamb being led to the slaughter. He was quiet, as a sheep is quiet while its wool is being cut. He never opened his mouth.

Men took him away roughly and unfairly. He died without children to continue his family. He was put to death. He was punished for the sins of my people. He was assigned a grave with the wicked, and with the rich in his death. He had done nothing wrong. He had never lied. But it was the Lord who decided to crush him and make him suffer. So, the Lord made his life a penalty offering.

But he will see his descendants and live a long life. He will complete the things the Lord wants him to do. He will suffer many things in his soul. But then, he will see life and be satisfied. My good servant will make people right with God. He carried away their sins. For this reason, I will make him a great man among people. He will share in all things with those who are strong.

He willingly gave his life. He was treated like a criminal. But he carried away the sins of many people. And he asked forgiveness for those who sinned." [1]

Ready for the stunner?

That was written 700 years before Jesus was born, yet, today, it reads like it could be His biography.

---

1. Isaiah 53:2-12

The level of specificity God uses in these prophecies is miraculous. Others predicted that the Messiah will be born of a virgin[2], will be born in the tiny town of Bethlehem[3], will be a miracle worker[4], and more. Does that sound like anyone you know?

In retrospect, God left no real room for doubt as to the identity of the Messiah. That said, we must keep in mind that these prophecies were delivered hundreds of years before Christ. The message was there, but the people did not yet have the perspective to see it clearly.

Speaking of clear vision, anyone who has ever had an appointment with an eye doctor knows it usually involves a "Snellen test." That's the classic eye chart with lines of letters that begin very large at the top and successively decrease in size with each row down. The patient reads aloud letters in each row, starting with the largest and then down to the smallest. The smallest row of letters the patient can read accurately is used to determine the quality of their eyesight. For instance, if the patient can read the most miniature letters on the chart, they'd have 20/20 vision.

After the patient completes the test using the naked eye, the doctor often runs a second test, using various lenses to aid the patient's vision. The doctor flips through the lenses, asking, "Which one helps you see clearer? This one (lens one) or this one (lens two)." By process of

---

2. Isaiah 7:14.

3. Micah 5:1

4. Isaiah 35:5

elimination, the doctor can determine which are the correct lenses for the patient.

Interestingly, the patient gets to experience in real-time how the various lenses change their perspective. The letters on the chart don't change, but they can look completely different, depending on which lens is aiding their vision. Of course, the letters have been there all along, but some that the patient couldn't previously recognize with the naked eye are now seen as clear as day.

Do you realize that the problem of sin and our inability to solve it ourselves is like a Spiritual Snellen Test?

When we face these things, our understanding of the resurrection bursts into focus. In other words, the F.A.C.T.S. establish *that* Jesus rose from the dead; the problem of sin and our inability to solve it explains *why* Jesus rose from the dead. What was once blurry and unrecognizable has become sharp and evident.

Now that we have the proper lens aiding our vision, prophecies in the Bible delivered hundreds of years before Jesus was born suddenly make perfect sense. Check this out:

- **We are all sinners** - *We all have wandered away like sheep. Each of us has gone his own way.*[5]

- **Sin can't exist in the presence of God, so unless we can**

---

5. Isaiah 53:6

remove our sin, we must be separated from God (in hell)
- Your iniquities have made a separation between you and your God, and your sins have hidden his face from you so that he does not hear.[6]

- **We can't save ourselves. Trying to get right with God in our own power is futile.** *Can the Ethiopian change his skin or the leopard, his spots? Then you also can do good to those who are accustomed to evil and even trained to do it.*[7]

- **No amount of good deeds can remove the stain of sin -** *"All of us have become like one who is unclean, and all of our righteous acts are like filthy rags; we all shrivel up like a leaf, and like the wind, our sins sweep us away."*[8]

- **Those who can't save themselves need a Savior. Jesus is our Savior!** *"My good servant will make people right with God. He carried away their sins. He willingly gave his life. He was treated like a criminal. But he carried away the sins of many people. And he asked forgiveness for those who sinned.*[9]

---

6. Isaiah 59:2

7. Jeremiah 13:23

8. Isaiah 64:6

9. Isaiah 53:11

• **Jesus suffered, was crucified, and died as punishment for our sins. Yet, today, He's alive and satisfied.** *He died without children to continue his family. He was put to death. He was punished for the sins of my people. But he will see his descendants and live a long life. He will complete the things the Lord wants him to do. He will suffer many things in his soul. But then, he will see life and be satisfied.* [10]

Can you see it? Is it coming into focus for you?

The purpose of the resurrection is to serve as a substitute for our sins

So, the Lord made his life a penalty offering. He took our suffering on him and felt our pain for us. We saw his suffering. We thought God was punishing him. But he was pierced for the wrong things we did. He was crushed for the evil things we did. The punishment, which made us well, was given to him. And we are healed because of his wounds. He was punished for the sins of my people. He had done nothing wrong. He had never lied. But it was the Lord who decided to crush him and make him suffer. [11]

---

10. Isaiah 53:8-11

11. Isaiah 53 misc.

We know that we, by nature, are utterly incapable of living a sin-free life. But, thank God, it's not about what we can do. It's about what Jesus accomplished through the resurrection! He took the punishment that we rightly deserve for our sins. He took it all, and by His wounds, we are healed. His suffering, death, and resurrection serve as a substitute - or penalty offering - for the sins of all believers.

Do you know what that sounds like to me? Good News! The best, most important news in history, to be more precise. We know this isn't something we can earn on our own merit, so, how exactly do we receive this gift? Let's get out our spiritual tape measures and get back to work...

***

Chapter 12

THE GOOD
NEWS

"The instructions said to preheat the oven at 180 degrees. I'm not sure I'll try this recipe again. Turning the oven upside down was a real backbreaker."

I've heard it said that there is some grain of truth in every joke. This one certainly has it, poking fun at peoples' propensity to mistakes despite seemingly clear directions. Of course, God, the source of all truth, knows this. When it comes to our most crucial problem, I'm thankful that He has preserved for us clear instructions in His Word. Here, we have the Son of God essentially teaching a masterclass on God's solution to our problem:

> *"There was a man of the Pharisees named Nicodemus,*
> *a ruler of the Jews. This man came to Jesus at night and*
> *said to Him, 'Rabbi, we know that You are a teacher*

who comes from God; for no one can do these signs that you do unless God is with Him.' Jesus answered and said to him, **'Most assuredly, I say to you, unless one is born again, he cannot see the kingdom of God.'** *Nicodemus said to Him, 'How can a man be born when he is old? Can he enter a second time into his mother's womb and be born?' Jesus answered, 'Most assuredly, I say to you, unless one is born of water and the Spirit, he cannot enter the kingdom of God. That which is born of the flesh is flesh, and that which is born of the Spirit is spirit. Do not marvel that I said to you, 'you must be born again.' The wind blows where it wishes, and you hear the sound of it, but cannot tell where it comes from and where it goes. So is everyone who is born of the Spirit.' Nicodemus answered and said to Him, 'How can these things be?' Jesus answered and said to him, 'Are you the teacher of Israel, and do not know these things? Most assuredly, I say to you, 'We speak what We know and testify what We have seen, and you do not receive Our witness. If I have told you earthly things and you do not believe, how will you believe if I tell you heavenly things? No one has ascended to heaven but He who came down from heaven, that is, the Son of Man who is in heaven. Just as Moses lifted up the [bronze] serpent in the desert [on a pole], so must the Son of Man be lifted up [on the cross], that whoever believes in Him should not perish, but have eternal life [after physical death, and will actually live forever].* **For God so loved the world that he gave His one and only Son, that whoever believes in Him shall** *not perish but have eternal life. For God did not send His Son into the world to condemn the world, but to save the world through Him. Whoever believes in Him is not condemned, but whoever does not believe stands condemned already because they have not believed in the name of God's one and only Son.'"* [1]

God loves us so much that he gave His beloved Son as a penalty offering for the punishment that we rightfully deserve. This is an incredible demonstration of the grace of God. Grace is an oft-misunderstood concept, so, let's break it down. Grace refers to unmerited favor. Unmerited means "not deserved," and favor means "an act of kindness beyond what is due or usual." In other words:

The resurrection of Jesus is the ultimate act of kindness that we do not deserve.

This principle of grace is so critical that it's mentioned in the Bible over 150 times. It is by grace that we are saved from the punishment we deserve. Think about it; if we could save ourselves from God's judgment, why would God have sent Jesus to suffer, be crucified, and rise again? As a backup plan in case our own way doesn't work out? Of course not. We cannot earn our way into heaven. Rather, freedom from sin and, therefore, an eternity spent with God is there to be *received.*

---

1. John 3:1-18

So, how exactly do we receive it? **We must be born again**. "*Unless one is born again, he cannot see the kingdom of God.*" And how exactly are we born again? **We must believe in Jesus**.

Take note of the language because this is critical. We must believe in Jesus. There is a difference between belief *that* someone exists and belief *in* someone. The Bible is clear that the mere belief that Jesus exists isn't the standard: "*You believe there is one God. Good! Even the demons believe that — and shudder.*" [2]

Rather, we must believe **in** Him. What does that entail?

- I'm a sinner who deserves to be separated from God in hell.

- I cannot save myself from this just punishment.

- God raised Jesus from the dead to serve as a substitute for my sins.

- Jesus is the Son of God. I make Him my Lord and Savior.

Putting your belief in Jesus means you're giving up the illusion that you can save yourself. Instead, you're putting your complete faith in Him and what He accomplished on the cross. By definition, believing in Jesus means you believe that He alone can save you. There is no backup plan if you believe in Him. Think about getting engaged to your husband or wife, "Listen... I believe in you. I want to get married. I am going to make an online dating profile and keep seeing other

---

2. James 2:19

people just in case things don't work out between us. But I believe in you." How would that go over?

Friend, you don't need to be an expert on every facet of this. It's a lifelong endeavor. But if you believe in your heart that Jesus is Lord, God raised Him from the dead, and He alone can save you, you'll be born again spiritually. The Holy Spirit led the Apostle Paul to sum it up masterfully:

> *"Among these [unbelievers] we all once lived in the passions of our flesh [our behavior governed by the sinful self], indulging the desires of human nature [without the Holy spirit] and [the impulses] of the [sinful] mind. We were, by nature, children [under the sentence] of [God's] wrath, just like the rest [of mankind]. But God, being rich in mercy, because of His great and wonderful love with which He loved us, even when we were [spiritually] dead and separated from Him because of our sins, He made us [spiritually] alive together with Christ (for by His grace - His undeserved favor and mercy - you have been saved from God's judgment). And He raised us up together with Him [when we believed], and seated us with Him in the heavenly places, [because we are] in Christ Jesus, [and He did this] so that in the ages to come, He might [clearly] show the immeasurable and unsurpassed riches of His grace in [His] kindness toward us in Jesus Christ [by providing for our redemption].* **For it is by grace that you have been saved through faith.** *And this [salvation] is not of yourselves but it is the gift of God; not as a result of*

[your] works, so that no one will be able to boast or take credit in any way [for his salvation]."³

There it is.

The only solution to our problem of sin is to be born again. That happens when we believe in Jesus alone as our Lord and Savior. It's a free gift from God that we don't deserve and cannot earn.

In other words, salvation comes from God's grace through our faith in Christ alone.

***

---

3. Ephesians 2: 3-9

Chapter 13

IT IS FINISHED

Here, we find Jesus drawing his final breath on the cross:

> *"After this, Jesus,* **knowing that all things were now accomplished, that the scripture might be fulfilled,** *said, 'I thirst!' Now a vessel full of sour wine was sitting there; and they filled a sponge with sour wine, put it on hyssop, and put it to his mouth. So, when Jesus had received the sour wine, He said, '**It is finished!**' And bowing His head, He willingly gave up His spirit.* [1]

Jesus declared, *"It is finished!"* when He knew He had accomplished His mission. His mission was to do the will of His Father in fulfillment of the scriptures. *"Jesus said to them, 'My food is to do the will of Him who sent Me and to completely finish His work... For I have come down from heaven, not to do My own will, but to do the will of Him*

---

1. John 19:28-30

who sent Me... For this is My Father's will and purpose, that everyone who sees the Son and believes in Him [as Savior] will have eternal life, and I will raise him up [from the dead] on the last day." [2]

It is the will and purpose of the Father that no one who believes in Jesus as Savior would perish. That's exactly what Jesus accomplished through the cross. So, *"if the Son sets you free, you will be free indeed."* [3]

The Good News of Jesus Christ is that there is no condemnation, but only eternal life and everlasting joy awaiting those who believe in Him!

Another word for good news is Gospel. The Good News (or Gospel) refers to the death and resurrection of Jesus Christ as our substitute for our sins. When a person trusts Jesus alone for the forgiveness of sins and for the gift of eternal life, they're saved from the judgment they rightfully deserve from God (born again).

The Gospel is the next stone laid in reference to our Chief Cornerstone. We've taken the next logical step in our faith:

Since Jesus is the Son of God, my view of the Bible is based on what <u>He</u> taught about it. He taught that the Bible is the authoritative Word of God. Therefore, my #1 priority is to live in agreement with what it says.

---

2. John 4: 34, John 6: 38, 40.

3. John 8:36

What is says is, absolutely no sin can exist in heaven, but absolutely every person on Earth is a sinner. The Good News is, Jesus willingly suffered, died, and rose again to remove the sins of believers. Therefore, I've ditched all my own efforts and put my belief in Jesus alone as the solution.

Friend, we never know when our time on this Earth is up, which is why the problem of sin is so dire. If you've already been born again, right now is the perfect time to pray for someone you love who isn't. With that person in mind, we pray that: [4]

- The Lord would send believers across their path.

- God would plow up the hard ground of their heart using whatever means and circumstances He sees fit.

- The Holy Spirit would prepare their heart to receive the message of salvation.

- There would be a removal of their spiritual "blindness."

- God would graciously give them an "ear" to hear and respond to His voice.

If you've not yet accepted Jesus Christ as your Lord and Savior, there is quite literally no better time to do so than right now. Taste and see that He is good. If you haven't yet, it's time to ditch any efforts to get right with God on your own merit. Your ticket to freedom is

---

4. Victory Church, Middlefield, CT, How to Pray for the Lost.

putting your faith in Jesus alone. It's not about your good deeds or anything noble you've done; it's about what He accomplished on the cross. If you're ready, you can pray this sinner's prayer and change your life right now:

Sinner's Prayer

Lord God, I'm a sinner. I'm sorry, and I'm asking for your forgiveness. Jesus, I believe that You died on the cross for my sins, and that you defeated death by rising again. I'm turning away from my sins, and I invite you into my heart, into my life. I trust you fully, and I make you my Lord and Savior. I will never be the same. In Jesus' mighty name. Amen.

If you've just given your life to Jesus, I want to congratulate you. You're in for the ride of your life. And you're in the right place because we have more faith-building to do. Let's go.

***

Part 3 Review

Let's recap what we know:

1. The Authoritative Word of God says sin is the single most crucial problem in your life and mine. Unless we can somehow remove our sins, we rightfully will live our afterlives separated from God... in hell.

2. When it comes to the problem of sin, relying on yourself and what you can do is about as effective as you repairing the Titanic with a mop bucket and a roll of duct tape.

3. The purpose of the resurrection is to serve as a substitute for our sins.

4. The only solution to our problem of sin is to be born again. That happens when we believe in Jesus alone as our Lord and Savior.

5. The Good News of Jesus Christ is that there is no condemnation, but only eternal life, and everlasting joy awaiting those who believe in Him!

Bottom line #3: You must be born again. The Gospel is our gift from God.

PART 4: WHO IS GOD?

Chapter 14

SOFT-SERVE SALVATION?

PART 4 - WHO IS GOD?

The original Pinkberry Frozen Yogurt (froyo) restaurant opened in January 2005 and quickly exploded in popularity. It gained a cult following amongst celebrities and became a trendy must-visit spot in Los Angeles. With so many people driving across the city and waiting in lines of 20-30 minutes, Pinkberry was dubbed "the taste that launched 1,000 parking tickets." [1]

Pinkberry sparked a nationwide soft serve "froyo" craze, with froyo restaurants popping up on seemingly every corner. Competitors like 16 handles, Froyo World, Kiwi Spoon, and Sweet Frog jumped into the market to capitalize on the demand.

---

1. LA Times- 8/4/06.

One of the primary appeals of these soft serve froyo restaurants is the level of customization that is literally at the customer's fingertips. The yogurt dispensers and topping bars are generally self-serve, so, the customer is in control. The pricing is calculated by weight, allowing the customer to fill their cup with exactly as many yogurt flavors and toppings as they so choose.

Some may prefer just one flavor of yogurt, and others may prefer a little of every flavor. Then there's my youngest daughter, who gets about a thimble-full of frozen yogurt and loads up the rest of her cup with candy from the toppings bar. The point is that the potential combinations are endless, and they all lead to the same place – a full belly. These restaurants often market themselves as frozen yogurt done "your way."

When it comes to froyo, having it "your way" can be wonderful. But what about when it comes to our faith in the living God? Popular sentiment in our culture today is that all religions lead to heaven, and you can indeed have God "your way." But there's a problem. Jesus Christ, the Son of God, says He's the way. "Woke" thinking in our culture today says personal experience is king, and you must live "your truth." But Jesus, the king of kings, says He's the truth. And finally, the internet glorifies "living your best life," but Jesus, the Living God, says He's the life.

What I'm saying is, being born again through the Good News of Jesus Christ is not a way to heaven, it's the only way to heaven.

This declaration might sound closed-minded to some, which would be understandable if it were Christians who decided that Jesus was the only way. But it wasn't a Christ-follower who said it; it was Christ Himself. So, here, Jesus explains to His followers the way to heaven:

> *Thomas said to him, 'Lord, we don't know where you are going, so, how can we know the way?' Jesus answered, 'I am the way, the truth, and the life. No one comes to the Father except through me.'*[2]

No one comes to the Father except through Jesus. God has made this concept so clear throughout His Word that to read the Bible and miss it enters into "What Won't Stanley Notice" territory. Fellow fans of one of my favorite T.V. shows, The Office, will recognize that reference. One of the characters, Stanley, is so consumed by his cross-word puzzle that he fails to notice anything going on around him. He accidentally drinks his colleague Jim's orange juice rather than his own hot coffee and does not react to it. When Jim sees this, he and the rest of the staff decide to test Stanley's obliviousness. They wear various costumes, replace his computer monitor with a cardboard cutout, discuss an office location on the planet Jupiter, and even bring a pony into the office. Stanley never looks up from his crossword puzzle and notices none of it. The only thing that grabs his attention is when the clock hits 5 PM so that he can hurry out of the office.

Stanley was so distracted by his own interest that he missed the entire purpose of being in the office – to work! It requires that level of

---

2. John 14:5-6

preoccupation with your personal desires to miss what God says about Jesus being the only way to heaven. In case *"I am the way"* leaves any uncertainty, we find this principle reiterated throughout scripture:

*"So, Jesus said again, 'I assure you and most solemnly say to you, I am the Door for the sheep [leading to life]. All who came before Me [as false messiahs and self-appointed leaders] are thieves and robbers, but the [true] sheep did not hear them. **I am the Door; anyone who enters through Me will be saved** [and will live forever], and will go in and out [freely], and find pasture (spiritual security).'"*[3]

*"This Jesus is the stone which was despised and rejected by you, the builders, but which became the Chief Cornerstone. **And there is salvation in no one else;** for there is no other name under heaven that has been given among people by which we must be saved [for God has provided the world no alternative for salvation]."*[4]

No one who denies the Son has the Father; *whoever acknowledges the Son has the Father also.*[5]

We accept human testimony, but God's testimony is greater because it is the testimony of God, which he has given about his Son. Whoever believes in the Son of God accepts this testimony. Whoever does not believe God has made him out to be a liar, because they have not believed the tes-

---

3. John 10:7-9

4. Acts 4:11-12

5. 1 John 2:23

timony God has given about his Son. **And this is the testimony, God has given us eternal life, and this life is in His Son. Whoever has the Son has life; whoever does not have the Son of God does not have life.** [6]

"Therefore, my friends, I want you to know that through Jesus, the forgiveness of sins is proclaimed to you. **Through him, everyone who believes is set free from every sin, a justification you were not able to obtain under the law of Moses."** [7]

In the Bible, Jesus is referred to as God's "one and only Son." That means He is "one of a kind." One of a kind refers to a person regarded as precious, special, exceptional, beyond ordinary, or unequaled. God didn't send His one and only Son as a penalty offering for our sins to be one of the myriads of options for us. Jesus is the way, the truth, and the life. It's for this reason that the Apostles, led by the Holy Spirit, so fiercely protected the Gospel (Good News) of Jesus Christ. Let's explore.

***

6. 1 John 5:9-12

7. Acts 13:38-39

Chapter 15

A DIFFERENT GOSPEL, WHICH IS REALLY NO GOSPEL AT ALL

C ounterfeit medication is big business, with the market valued at 200+ billion dollars per year. These fake medications are produced and sold with the intent to deceptively represent their origin, authenticity, or effectiveness. Often, the packaging looks very similar to the actual medicine, making the fraud challenging to detect. The drugs may contain incorrect quantities of active ingredients or even no active ingredients at all. They typically have little to no actual health value to the patient. [1]

Counterfeiters peddle all types of fake medicines — anti-inflammatories, birth control, anti-anxiety pills, HIV treatments, and almost everything in between. This fraud adds hundreds of millions of dollars to healthcare costs, and the effects can be deadly. For example, it's estimated that over 100,000 people per year die in sub-Saharan Africa because they're sold ineffective counterfeit malaria medication. It's evil.

In a particularly troubling report, the World Health Organization warned cancer patients about a counterfeit leukemia drug that contained nothing more than Tylenol. Can you imagine the gall of these counterfeiters? They're duping patients who are already battling a terminal disease. While the drugs may appear similar to the real thing based on surface-level comparisons, there is no actual benefit to the patient. Without the intervention of the true medicine, the patient will surely die from their terminal condition. Do you know what that's like?

Every religion on Earth other than the Good News of Jesus Christ.

---

1. Acri, Kristina M.L., and née Lybecker. "Executive Summary." *Pharmaceutical Counterfeiting: Endangering Public Health, Society and the Economy*. Fraser Institute, 2018. http://www.jstor.org/stable/resrep23987.3.

As a refresher: The Good News (Gospel) says there is no condemnation, but only eternal life and everlasting joy awaiting those who *believe in Jesus alone* as Savior. This refers to the death and resurrection of Jesus Christ as a substitute for our sins. So, when a person trusts Jesus alone for the forgiveness of sins and the gift of eternal life, they're saved from the judgment they rightfully deserve from God. They're born again.

In contrast, Pastor John MacArthur points to Romans 10:3 as the working definition of every false religion practiced by man:

> *Since they did not know the righteousness of God and sought to establish their own, they did not submit to God's righteousness.*

In other words, every other religion in the world is premised on the goal of getting right with God through some sort of human achievement. The achievement may be religious, moral, ceremonial, sacrificial, or otherwise, but it's all about humans earning their own righteousness. So, if you perform these ceremonies, or follow that rule, or get married in this temple, then you will be righteous and go to heaven. Or, more recently, if you're a "good person," then God surely owes you heaven, regardless of your religion.

But we've already established that salvation comes as a free gift from God (grace) for those who believe in Jesus alone as Savior (faith).

The Word of God affirms it plainly: "*By this gospel, you are saved.*" [2] Salvation cannot be earned by good works. Therefore, any Gospel outside the confines of grace alone by faith alone in Christ alone, is counterfeit.

The Bible addresses this issue in Paul's letter to the church in Galatia. The Apostle Paul had preached the Good News in Galatia. Evidently, there were "agitators" who later attempted to distort the Gospel by adding other Jewish religious laws and customs to it. Their message was faith in Jesus, plus, any number of human works required to be Holy. Therefore, salvation was no longer a free gift, but rather, something to be earned. The Biblical response is resounding:

> *I am astonished that you are so quickly deserting the one who called you to live in the grace of Christ and are turning to a different gospel –* **which is really no gospel at all.** *Evidently, some people are throwing you into confusion and are trying to pervert the gospel of Christ. But even if we or an angel from heaven should preach a gospel other than the one we preached to you, let them be under God's curse!* [3]

Wow. Tell us how you really feel, Holy Spirit. There's more:

> *You foolish Galatians! Who has bewitched you? Before your very eyes, Jesus Christ was clearly portrayed as crucified. I would like to learn one thing from you: Did you*

---

3. Galatians 1:6-8

receive the spirit by the works of the law (good deeds), or by believing what you heard? Are you so foolish? After beginning by means of the spirit, are you now trying to finish by means of the flesh? [4]

Grace alone, by faith alone, in Christ alone. This is the Good News of Jesus Christ. There is no other Gospel by which we can be saved. It's this truth that highlights one of the most damaging trends in our culture today.

In many circles, people believe that accepting all religions as equally true is loving. However, for followers of Christ, it's actually one of the most hateful things you could do.

Let's examine why...

***

---

4. Galatians 3:1-3

Chapter 16

EXCLUSIVELY INCLUSIVE GOOD NEWS

We know that the Good News of Jesus Christ is a supremely exclusive message, in that, there is only one way to remove our sins, get right with God, and spend eternity with Him in heaven. This flies in the face of the contemporary trend that "all roads lead to heaven." The fruit of this trend is a general indifference when it comes to God, in the name of "tolerance." Jesus Himself explained how damaging the idea that "all roads lead to heaven" is:

> *"Enter through the narrow gate. For wide is the gate and broad is the road that leads to destruction, and many*

*enter through it. But small is the gate and narrow is the
road that leads to life, and only a few find it."* [1]

Paradoxically, this supremely exclusive path to heaven is, in another
sense, supremely inclusive. Here's what I mean:

It's not that all roads lead to heaven; it's that all believers have access to the one road that does.

The Gospel is a covenant that God has made with every believer in
history. The Bible says that <u>all believers</u> are children of God through
faith. *"There is neither Jew nor Gentile, neither slave nor free, nor is there
male and female, for you are all one in Christ Jesus."* (Gal 3:26)

That's about as inclusive as it gets. And the assignment that Jesus
gave His followers after He rose from the dead is rooted in this truth.
Essentially, He's saying that since there is only one way to get right
with God, we need to share that way with everyone on Earth.

> *"All authority has been given to Me in heaven and on
> earth.* **Go therefore, and make disciples of all na-
> tions,** *baptizing them in the name of the Father and of
> the Son and of the Holy Spirit, teaching them to observe
> all things that I have commanded you; and lo, I am
> with you always, even to the end of the age."* [2]

---

1. Matthew 7:13

2. Matthew 28:18-19

Go and make disciples of all nations is one of the last things Jesus said before ascending back up to heaven. We *must* share the Good News of Jesus Christ to fulfill this assignment. Sharing the Good News is not only obedient to the Word of God, but also, the most loving thing you can do for someone else.

Think about it as if every person on the planet had terminal cancer and you had the one perfect cure for it. You'd meet some people who had resorted to counterfeit medications and others living in outright denial that they're sick at all. Would it be loving to smile at them and let them go their own way when you know they're headed toward disaster? Would that type of "tolerance" be just? Of course not. Thus, it would be incumbent on everyone who has the perfect cure to share it with those who don't.

It's the same with the Good News. Every person on Earth has the terminal condition of sin, and belief in Jesus is the only cure. Therefore, it's incumbent on all believers to share the Good News. This is the next stone laid in relation to our Chief Cornerstone:

I put my belief in Jesus alone because He said, "I am the way, the truth, and the life. No one comes to the Father except through me." Therefore, the single most loving thing I can do for someone else is to share with them the Good News.

Now, when we share the Good News, we don't bring the message on our own authority. Why would anyone listen if it were a message based simply on human opinion? No, the Bible says that we are *"ambas-*

sadors for Christ, as though God were making His appeal through us."
[3] Therefore, we share the Good News on God's authority. And Jesus clearly spells out who the God of the Bible is:

> *Go therefore, and make disciples of all nations,* **baptizing them in the name of the Father and of the Son and of the Holy Spirit.**

There is a detail in this command that is absolutely crucial to understand. **Jesus did *not* say to baptize them in the *names* of the Father, and of the Son, and of the Holy Spirit.** He used the singular: **name.** *Baptize them in the* **name** *of the Father, and of the Son, and of the Holy Spirit.* Why?

Because there is only one true living God – the God of the Bible. He exists eternally in three co-equal persons: God the Father, God the Son, and God the Holy Spirit. [4]

This is what's referred to as the Trinity. We know that there is only One God:

> *"This is what the Lord says — Israel's King and Re-*
> *deemer, the Lord Almighty; I am the first and I am the*
> *last; apart from me, there is no God. Who then is like*

---

4. Allen Parr, "The Trinity Explained," YouTube video.

me? Let him proclaim it... I am God and there is no other; I am God, and there is none like me." [5]

However, we see a plurality within our One God dating back to before the universe began. We need not go past the very first chapter in the very first book of the Bible to begin to see it:

> *"Then God said, '**Let us make mankind in our image, in our likeness**, so that they may rule over the fish in the sea and the birds in the sky, over the livestock and the wild animals, and over all the creatures that move along the ground.'"* [6]

The one true living God, the God of the Bible, exists eternally in three co-equal persons. If that is a concept that challenges you intellectually, welcome to the club! It should not be a surprise to us that we can't fully grasp an infinite God. But God has revealed to us through His Word the truth of the doctrine of the Holy Trinity.

Without an understanding of the Trinity, we can't truly understand God's nature and what Jesus accomplished on the cross. The Trinity is the next "stone" we lay in relation to the Chief Cornerstone. Let's keep going so we can have more clarity on this...

---

5. Isaiah 44:6, 46:9 NIV.

6. Genesis 1:26

***

Chapter 17

DIVINE CHILD ABUSE?

Imagine walking out of the grocery store and discovering that a teenage driver has crashed into your car in the parking lot. Thankfully, no one is injured, but the impact dented your bumper and cracked your rear windshield. The driver is shaken up and is sincerely apologizing. He's in a jam. He doesn't have two nickels to rub together, and it's clearly going to be expensive to repair the damages. It's money he doesn't have.

Suddenly, a random bystander walks over to console the driver. The bystander tells the driver not to worry about the cost of repairs and that he's free to go. The driver is shocked and relieved. He thanks the bystander for the kindness, gets back in his car, and drives away. Meanwhile, you're the one left with the damaged car.

Does that seem right to you? Would you go and thank the random bystander for making that choice for you? Of course not. You're the aggrieved party. We know inherently that *only the one who is owed can forgive a debt.* The bystander had no right to do that on your behalf.

Do you realize that every time we sin, we're sinning against our perfectly holy God?

That's why only God can forgive our sins. The damage is against Him.

That may sound unusual to you, so, let's get out our spiritual tape measure and measure it by the Word of God. First, we see in Genesis 39 when Joseph is seduced by his boss's wife. Joseph tells her, "Your husband has treated me great. He's kept nothing from me except for you, because you're his wife. How then could I do this great evil and *sin against God?*" [1] We see this also in 2nd Samuel after David had committed adultery and murder. *"Against You, You only, have I sinned And done that which is evil in Your sight, So that You are justified when You speak [Your sentence] And faultless in Your judgment."* [2] [3]

Obviously, those sins hurt other people too, but the Word of God shows us that all sin is ultimately against God Himself. It's His laws we're breaking and therefore, it's God who bears the damages. Only He can release us from that debt.

---

1. Genesis 39:9-paraphrased.

2. Psalm 51:4.

3. Examples from compellingtruth.org

Now, this begs the question: if the damage is against God, why did He send His poor Son, Jesus to pay the price for our sins? It seems like an unbelievably harsh thing to do to anyone, let alone your own Son. How could He do that? I've even heard the resurrection referred to as child abuse by creative atheists.

These questions and objections indicate a misunderstanding of the Trinity. If we don't believe in the Trinity as defined in the Bible (Father, Son, and Holy Spirit), we can't know who God is. If we don't know who God is, we cannot grasp the Good News.

The terminology that trips many people up is Jesus as the "Son of God." Many take that to mean God the Father created Jesus. But that's not at all what it says in the Bible. If Jesus were a created being, that would mean that He is some sort of lesser or diminished God. But the Word could not be more clear that there is only one God.

No, Jesus was not created. He is an uncreated Creator. He was there "in the beginning" and everything that has been created has been created through Him. The first line in the Bible says, "*In the beginning, God created the heavens and the earth.*" [4] Now, look at the parallel in the first line in the Gospel of John: "*In the beginning was the Word (Jesus), and the Word was with God, and the Word was God. He was with God in the beginning. Through Him, all things were made; without him, nothing was made that has been made.*" [5]

---

4. Genesis 1:1

5. John 1:1

There is no perfect comparison because there is no other being like God, but a better way to think about the "Son of God" role is to consider the relationship between a husband and wife. They are both fully human and equally human, yet, they play different roles in the marriage. Likewise, The Father, The Son, and the Holy Spirit are all fully God and equally God, yet, they play different roles in the being of the one true God. The Bible affirms that Jesus is fully God, and at the same time, The Father is fully God, and at the same time, the Holy Spirit is fully God. Thus, we have one Holy God who exists eternally in three co-equal persons.

Now, in the light of the Trinity, we can understand why the Bible tells us that God *is* love. [6] How could He *be* love if, before creating the universe, He was alone? Love is something that one person feels for another.

God *is* love because the three distinct persons of the Trinity have loved one another for eternity.

When we consider this dynamic, it sheds the Good News in a whole new light. Jesus isn't some diminished being that the true God created and cruelly sent down to take the fall for humanity. Jesus is fully God, one of the three persons of the Trinity. When God gave His only Son to save us, He literally gave Himself. That's not child abuse; that's a more profound love than we can fathom.

---

6. 1 John 4:7

I want you to think about someone you love deeply — a spouse, child, parent, friend, whoever it may be. What would it take for you to voluntarily send them to experience hell on Earth?

Now, consider that your love for this person has grown over the course of months, years, or decades. As deep as that love feels to you, the three persons of the Trinity have loved one another *for eternity.* They are literally one Being! And God the Father was willing to send God the Son as a penalty offering to remove from us our sins.

How much must our God love us that He would voluntarily do that? God the Father voluntarily sent God the Son, and God the Son willingly came to give his life for you and me. Therefore, the Bible urges us to *"grasp how wide and long and high and deep is the love of Christ, and to know that this love surpasses knowledge, so that you may be filled with all the fullness of God."*[7]

God does not wish that anyone should perish. His love surpasses understanding. We were dead in our sins, separated from our Creator, but He gave Himself, His only Son, to save the world. We have a loving heavenly Father and Savior. This is the next stone laid in relation to the Chief Cornerstone:

I share the Good News, not by any human authority, but as an ambassador for the one true living God.

---

7. Ephesians 3:18

He exists eternally in three persons – The Father, The Son, and The Holy Spirit.

***

PART 4 RECAP

L et's review what we know:

1. Being born again through the Good News of Jesus Christ is not a way to heaven, it's the only way to heaven.

2. Affirming all religions as equally true is one of the most hateful things a Christian could do.

3. It's not that all roads lead to heaven, it's that all believers have access to the one road that does. Therefore, we must share the Good News with all nations.

4. There is one true living God – the God of the Bible. He exists eternally in three co-equal persons: God the Father, God the Son, and God the Holy Spirit.

5. God *is* love because the three distinct persons of the Trinity have loved one another for eternity.

Bottom Line #4 is, we must share the Good News because it is the only way to heaven. We share it as ambassadors of the God of the Bible, who exists eternally as The Father, the Son, and the Holy Spirit.

PART 5: BURN THE SHIPS

Chapter 18

AM I SAVED?

PART 5 - BURN THE SHIPS

The Aztec Empire dominated what is now central and southern Mexico from the mid-14th century until 1521. The empire began as an alliance of tribes following a civil war, and warfare remained deeply engrained within the Aztec culture. Children learned how to handle weapons and also mastered combat skills from a young age, and boys were taught that their purpose as men was to die gloriously in battle. The Aztecs worshipped dozens of false gods and believed that warriors killed in battle would be reincarnated as hummingbirds.

The Aztecs used their battle prowess to gain territory, controlling over 200,000 square miles and 11 million people at their height of power. With each neighboring tribe conquered, the Aztecs expanded their tax base and their pool of eligible soldiers. The conquered tribes were left to govern themselves, so long as they paid taxes to the empire, supplied warriors when needed for battle and added the Aztec false gods to the local collection of false deities. Eventually, the Aztecs were collecting tribute from nearly 400 cities under the empire's control. [1]

Meanwhile, Hernan Cortes was born some 5,500 miles away in the town of Medellin, Spain. Cortes was the conquistador who would conquer the Aztec Empire and claim Mexico for the crown of Spain. Cortes had just 11 ships, about 500 men, 13 horses, and a small number of cannons under his command for the conquest. On the way to the Aztec capital, Cortes made alliances with rival indigenous tribes to grow his army and improve their odds of victory. This strategy proved effective, as many tribes were eager to destroy the Aztecs and remove the tax burden imposed by the empire. On August 13, 1521, the Aztec capital was captured for Spain and re-named Mexico City.

Despite having almost no military experience, Cortes made a brilliant move to lead his army to victory. Upon landing on the shores of Mexico, Cortes ordered that their own fleet of ships be burned. The soldiers watched their only chance of retreat sink to the bottom of the Atlantic. The message was clear: they would succeed in their conquest, or they would die trying. The only way they were leaving Mexico alive would be in the ships of conquered Aztecs.

The principle here is, when you're 100% all in on something, there is no backup plan.

This means that if you have truly put your belief in Jesus alone as your Savior, there is no backup plan.

---

1. Worldhistory.org

Friend, is your trust in Jesus alone? Or is it in Jesus plus something else? Because if you believe Jesus is a way to be saved and not the only way to be saved, you don't actually believe the Good News. To be saved, we must burn our ships and be completely sold out for Jesus.

The Bible tells us to examine ourselves to see if we are in the faith. [2] It says to test ourselves in this regard. By now, you know that our faith is not merely based on "feelings," which are deceitful and thus, change over time. Saying that you "feel" like you've been saved isn't necessarily a great indicator of whether or not you actually have. Rather, the best evidence that someone has been saved can be summed up in one word – **change**.

Your life changes after being saved. What you want changes after being saved. This is one of the most misunderstood truths of Christianity.

A changed lifestyle doesn't cause someone to be saved; it's an effect of being saved.

In other words, it's only belief in Jesus that can save us, so if you don't honestly believe, your life won't change.

Jesus taught, *"Not everyone who says to me, 'Lord, Lord,' will enter the kingdom of heaven, but only the one who does the will of my Father*

---

2. 2 Cor 13:5

who is in heaven."[3] Therefore, the act of praying the sinner's prayer to accept Jesus into your heart isn't some on-demand salvation button. Think about it; if you pray the sinner's prayer and then go on living exactly as you were before, what would make you think you've been saved?

You used to enjoy partying and getting drunk, and then you decide to pray, but you still do it. You were promiscuous before, and now you say you believe in Jesus, and you're still promiscuous. You didn't go to church before, and then you pray, and now you only go on Christmas and Easter. You didn't read the Bible before, and you still don't. You idolized godless celebrities before, and you still want to be like them.

Friend, getting saved happens in an instant, but it's preceded and followed by a lifetime of change. The believer's life is transformed over time because God changes what we want.

When Jesus proclaimed the Good News, He told the people, "*The time has come. The Kingdom of God has come near. Repent and believe the good news.*"[4] To repent means to change! It means to turn away from your sinful ways and turn to the ways of God.

You repent when you turn from your own efforts and put your full belief in Jesus alone as Savior. Once you're saved, God will continue transforming you all your life. If you picture your life as a wheel, you'd be at the center, with each part of your life representing a spoke —

---

3. Matthew 7:21

4. Mark 1:15

your family, friends, faith, career, interests, etc. The transformation occurs once God is no longer a spoke on the wheel of your life. You move out of the center, and He moves in. When that happens, do you know what changes?

Everything. Literally, everything. Not all at once, but God loves you way too much to leave you the way He finds you.

When you make Jesus the Chief Cornerstone of your life, it means you build every facet of your life in relation to Him. Your marriage, raising your kids, who you spend time with, your work, your finances, your role models, the entertainment you consume — everything is ordered in relation to the Cornerstone.

Does this mean you magically become a perfect person? Of course not! We know we're sinners by nature. But when you step off the path of righteousness, God will reprimand you and get you back on track. My Pastor, Peter Leal Sr., compares this to the "rumble strips" we encounter on the highway. If you drift off course, those rumble strips will alert you that something is wrong, so that you can fix it in a hurry. So, likewise, when we inevitably fail in the ways of righteousness, God will jar us to get our attention and get us back on the path.

God changes what we want and how we want to live because, once saved, we're being prepared for eternity with Him. He's developing us into "an instrument for noble purposes, made holy, useful to the Master, and prepared to do any good work." Everything we do, other than sin, can be done for God's glory. And the ultimate expression of this "Kingdom work" done here on Earth is to fulfill our marching orders of sharing the Good News with all nations.

***

Chapter 19

KINGDOM WORK

Have you noticed that the topic of God seems to come up constantly in your conversations? Of course, it does. Why? Because once you've burnt your ships and put your full faith in Jesus, you're no longer living for yourself. You're living for Him. Your life revolves around Him. Your lifestyle will stick out because, as a believer, you are expressly and deliberately living differently than the world. You reject the ways of the world anytime they're not in agreement with the Word of God, which is constantly.

You won't even have to force the issue. When God is working on you and your lifestyle changes, the people around you notice. When you live with a concern for doing the will of God, people will want to know what has gotten into you. What do you have that they don't? It's your duty to share with them the Good News as an ambassador for the Father, the Son, and the Holy Spirit.

This implies that most unbelievers you interact with will have an objection or objections to the faith. That's a good thing! We should look at every objection from an unbeliever as the wonderful opportunity that it is.

Since Jesus is the truth, every objection to Jesus is a lie that can and will be crushed by the weight of the Word of God.

Realfaith.com has identified the top five objections to Christianity. Those who have left the church and those who were never part of the church share the same top five. Do any of these sound familiar to you?

1. The Christian faith and I have different views on social issues like abortion and gay marriage.

2. Some Christian groups are too intolerant.

3. I don't like how some Christian groups meddle in politics.

4. Many Christians are hypocrites.

5. There are lots of religions, and I'm not sure only one has to be the right way.

There are wonderful books that do a deep dive on specific objections like these. Personally, I think "Confronting Christianity" by Rebecca McLaughlin does a great job of it. But for our purposes, we'll focus on a glaring omission on the list. Your eyes do not deceive you.

Amazingly, not one of the top five objections to Christianity mentions Jesus!

We've come full circle and are back where we began, friend. The top objections to Christianity do not even address the structural integrity of the faith – the resurrection. So, it's no wonder that these objections materialize into spiritual whac-a-mole. Thankfully, only one question needs to be posed to begin a fruitful discussion on Christianity: **Fib, Dead, or God?** Both the believer and the skeptic must answer this question to explain any position relating to Christianity.

There have been objections against Jesus quite literally since He was born, and you can count on an ever-evolving list of complaints in your lifetime. Jesus Himself said that only a few will find the narrow gate that leads to heaven, so we should not be surprised by unbelief. The beautiful thing is, despite the standard that skeptics may seek to hold you to, you don't need to be a world-class expert on all things. So often, the skeptic will seek to place upon you the burden of proof to justify all Christians throughout history, all churches, all church practices, every wacky theory, and every question in their mind.

Respectfully, it is pointless for skeptics to share their opinion on Christ's followers before they've addressed Christ Himself. Blaming Christians or a particular church practice does not absolve the unbeliever from answering the question posed by Jesus nearly 2,000 years ago: **"Who do you say that I am?"**

Friend, you need not be able to explain everything under the sun, but you can absolutely explain why you're a Christ-follower. The declaration of faith we continue to build does precisely that for the believer. Let's keep going...

***

Chapter 20

PETER'S RESTAURANT

*P*eter's Restaurant is a local spot I frequent from time to time. I *can't say it's my favorite place, but it's the closest restaurant to my house, so I find myself there probably once a month. The food, the service, even the background music they play — it's all pretty good. Like any hometown restaurant, they have their "regulars" that always seem to be there, but I pretty much keep to myself. I just want to get a decent meal and be on my way. My schedule is crazy these days, so I appreciate that they usually turn around my order quickly. I can get in and get out in no time. Overall, it may not be my first choice, but supporting a local establishment feels good.*

At least it used to.

I've admittedly grown tired of Peter's Restaurant. I've put some thought into it, and I've decided to stop eating altogether. Part of the issue is that my spouse doesn't really like eating at Peter's. There are also a few items on their menu that I don't love. As for my kids, I'm going to have them stop eating for now as well. When they get older, I'll encourage them to try all sorts of restaurants. That way, they can pick and choose whichever menu items suit their personal tastes and preferences.

At this point in the story, I'm expecting you to be scratching your head in puzzlement. This scenario doesn't make a whole lot of sense, does it? This guy is unhappy with one local restaurant, so he and his family stop eating altogether. Obviously, they can't live like that. If this seems like a disproportionate reaction to you, I would agree.

Now, let's drop the "Restaurant" and put a "St." in front of Peter's. This is, unfortunately, an all-too-familiar story for places with names like St. Peter's. A person attends the church that happens to be closest to their home. They aren't particularly committed and are more like spectators than active participating members. Without both spouses on board, attendance is sporadic. The experience isn't fulfilling, and eventually, they become dissatisfied with the church for whatever reason. Rather than expanding their search to find a church they can commit to, they stop going altogether and have no church life. Of course, this means their children also have no church life. It's a disproportionate reaction! And just as one can't live without eating, a Christ-follower cannot live in isolation.

Think I'm overstating the importance of every believer being an active member of the local church? As always, we need to measure it by the Word. So, let's return to the most important question in history and pull back the curtain on the following verse:

*Simon Peter answered and said, '**You are the Christ, the Son of the living God.**' Jesus answered and said to him, 'Blessed are you, Simon son of Jonah, for flesh and blood has not revealed this to you, but My Father who is in heaven. And I tell you that you are Peter, and **on this rock, I will build my church**, and the gates of Hades will not overcome it [by preventing the resurrection of Christ].'"* [1]

The first thing Jesus does after affirming that He is God is to declare He will build His church.

He is the architect of the church and builds it upon the truth of His resurrection. Absolutely nothing can overcome it.

Does it get any clearer than that? There are, of course, legitimate situations that could prevent a believer from being a member of a church for a temporary period — a move, military, travel, living in a super remote area, etc. But suppose someone is intentionally choosing to be outside of the local church. In that case, it's an indicator that they say Jesus is a fib or dead. It would be asymmetrical to say that Jesus is God and not be a local church member.

---

1. Matthew 16:16-18

The Bible goes on to tell us that Jesus loves the church and that the church is the "bride of Christ." [2] Therefore, to claim Jesus as God but not attend a church is like saying, "Jesus, I love you, and I trust you alone, but I'm not a fan of your wife."

It's also disobedient. The Bible says, "*let us consider how we may spur one another on toward love and good deeds, **not giving up meeting together**, as some are in the habit of doing, but encouraging one another – and all the more as you see the Day approaching*." [3] There is no Biblical model to be "spiritual but not a church person." Instead, it's assumed that believers are part of their local church.

Finally, it's simply unwise. We, as believers, benefit from being members of the local church. God designed it that way. We all know that who we choose to surround ourselves with has an impact on our lives. As a believer, we must surround ourselves with other believers. John Macarthur describes it like the coals in your grill. They stay hot for a long time when they're situated together in that grill, but if you take one out on its own, it grows cold in a hurry.

You may have had a bad experience at your church in the past. The reality is that there is no perfect church. We know that because churches are made up of people, and every person on the planet is a sinner. There may not be a perfect church, but there is a proper church for every believer to belong.

---

2. Ephesians 5:25

3. Hebrews 10:25

Have you ever joined a fitness group that committed to working out together? Why is that effective? Because you have now become accountable to someone other than yourself. The principle applies even more so here. We need to be held accountable by other believers to maximize our gifts. We need to be present, not just as spectators but as active participants, serving others like a tool in God's hand. That's why it's called being "planted" in your church. You're there to grow in Christ.

The bottom line is that we need to be a part of a church community to live an effective Christian life.

***

Part 5 Recap

L et's recap what we know:

1. If you have truly put your belief in Jesus alone as your Savior, there is no backup plan.

2. A changed lifestyle doesn't *cause* someone to be saved, it's an *effect* of being saved. God loves you too much to leave you the way He found you.

3. Since Jesus is the truth, every objection to Jesus is a lie that can and will be crushed by the weight of the Word of God.

4. Not one of the Top 5 objections to Christianity mentions Jesus.

5. The first thing Jesus does after affirming He is God is to declare that He, as Chief Cornerstone, will build the church.

Bottom line #5 is, it is essential for us to be a part of a church community, in order to live an effective Christian life.

PART 6: CONCLUSION

Chapter 21

THE NEW MAN

PART 6 - CONCLUSION

There are over 100 million cars on the road that have been in an accident. In fact, about 25% of all the used cars for sale at any given time have had damage. That means there are deals to be had for savvy car buyers. Accident history that may have been unknown in the past is now easily accessible using services like CARFAX. Instead of taking a car for a mechanic's inspection, consumers can review this info with a couple of clicks of a mouse. They can even check how significant the damage was to the car, whether it was driven away from the scene or towed, etc.

Another factor for car buyers to consider is the title status. In many states, cars that have been in an accident receive a "branded title" that sticks with the vehicle forever. These titles essentially "brand" the cars as damaged goods – it's either they've been totaled or been rebuilt. Insurance companies use this information, and many will not insure a vehicle with a branded title.

The bottom line is, a car that has been in an accident is worth less than one that has not. Even if the damages are repaired entirely and are undetectable, it's worth less. Specifically, a car that has had severe damage in its past is worth about $1,700 less on average than a comparable vehicle with no accidents. Car buyers can use this information to their advantage in negotiating a good deal. [1]

I tell you all of this to make something absolutely clear to you, friend.

YOUR SOUL IS NOT REFURBISHED.

Putting your faith in Jesus Christ alone and being born again (saved) does <u>not</u> make you into an improved version of yourself. **You are literally a new creation**. Let's measure:

"*Therefore, **if anyone is in Christ, he is a new creation** [reborn and renewed by the Holy Spirit]; the old things [the previous moral and spiritual condition] have passed away.*"[2]

God gave me an up-close and personal refresher course on this principle during the writing of this book. I found myself in a season of pain – spiritual, emotional, mental pain. The kind of pain that woke me up at night and caused racing thoughts throughout the day.

---

1. Carfax.com

2. 2 Cor 5:17

What happened? I thought I was past this stuff.

As difficult as it is in the moment, the timing isn't terribly surpris-
ing. The express purpose of this book is to glorify God and advance
His kingdom. When we undertake kingdom work, it stands to reason
that we'd receive resistance from our spiritual enemies. The Bible tells
us, to "*Put on the full armor of God, so that you can take your stand
against the devil's schemes. For our struggle is not against flesh and
blood, but against the rulers, against the authorities, against the powers
of this dark world and against the spiritual forces of evil in the heavenly
realms.*" [3]

Thankfully, God has equipped us. "*For though we live in the world,
we do not wage war as the world does. The weapons we fight with are not
the weapons of the world. On the contrary, they have the divine power
to demolish strongholds. We demolish arguments and every proud thing
that sets itself up against the true knowledge of God.*" [4]

The reality is that the devil is a liar. Jesus calls Him the "Father of
lies." [5] He and his cronies will take a grain of truth and twist it to
make you miserable. And that's exactly what they were doing to me
as I began to write this book. They didn't even try to hide the timing.
The night after I started writing, I became plagued with thoughts that
I wasn't worthy and my family wasn't worthy. Old anxieties, irrational

---

3. Ephesians 6:13

4. 2 Cor 10:3-5

5. John 8:44

distress and in general, things that hadn't bothered me in years, came creeping back in.

So, where did I go? To the Word of God, of course. The Bible tells us there is safety in a multitude of counselors,[6] and that's one of the many beautiful things that come from membership in the local church. I had mentors, friends, and Pastors - all believers - who were willing to counsel me in love using the Word of God.

I also got into the Word on my own. I wish I could say I'm perfectly consistent with it 365 days a year, but I'm not. That said, when I'm in a season of pain, I rarely ever miss that "morning appointment" of prayer, reading the Word, and quiet time with God. That's why CS Lewis calls pain "God's megaphone." There is nothing quite like it to get our attention.

In the early morning of July 4th, I was reading Pastor Rick Warren's Daily Hope devotional. That day's devotional was about changing our thinking, and it referenced Ephesians 4:23. So, as usual, I opened my Bible to find the appropriate passage. First, I checked the top heading to get a reference point as to where I was. I could then flip to the right book, chapter, and verse.

Except this time, I didn't have to.

With over 1,200 pages in that Bible, I opened it to the exact page I was seeking. This was no personal accomplishment. I just grabbed

---

6. Proverbs 11:14

the Bible, opened it, and sat there, stunned. In the past, I would have thought, "that's unbelievable." But the truth is, it's not unbelievable; it's God. And as most people who serve the Lord can attest, there are certain situations where you know, "That could only be God."

As we've discussed, feelings change and can be deceitful. I felt unworthy to proclaim the Good News because the enemy was doing what he does best – lying. I was struggling with my past until that morning when I opened the Bible to this:

The New Man

This I say, therefore, and testify in the Lord, that you should no longer walk as the rest of the Gentiles walk, in the futility of their mind, having their understanding darkened, because of the ignorance that is in them, because of the blindness of their heart, who, being past feeling, have given themselves over to lewdness, to work all uncleanness with greediness.

But you have not so learned Christ, if indeed you have heard Him and have been taught by Him, at the truth is in Jesus: that you have put off, concerning your former conduct, the old man which grows corrupt according to the deceitful lusts, and be renewed in the spirit of your mind,

and that you <u>put on the new man which was</u> <u>created according to God, in true righteousness</u> <u>and holiness.</u> [7]

Friend, being born again does *not* improve the old you. The old you is dead. When you put your faith in Jesus, your old self *"was crucified with Him so that the body ruled by sin might be done away with, that we should no longer be slaves to sin — because anyone who has died has been set free from sin."*[8] Your spirit is a new creation, washed clean by the blood of Jesus! So, let's lay this final stone in relation to the Chief Cornerstone...

***

7. Ephesians 4:17-24

8. Romans 6:3-7

Chapter 22

WHO DO YOU SAY HE IS?

Who do you say He is?

This is it, friend. This is where the rubber meets the road. It's the most important question in history asked by the most important person in history. Every one of us will have our lives and our eternities determined by how we answer it, including those who choose not to answer at all.

Sadly, most people will dodge this question all their lives.

Instead, they'll focus on other things and "try to be a good person" as they simultaneously reject the source of all good.

In ethics, an evasion is an act that deceives by stating a true statement that is irrelevant or leads to a false conclusion. The top 5 objections mentioned earlier are Exhibit A:

- The Christian faith and I have different views on social issues like abortion and gay marriage.

- I don't like how some Christian groups meddle in politics.

- Many Christians are hypocrites.

- There are lots of religions, and I'm not sure only one has to be the right way.

- Some Christian groups are too intolerant.

That's not an answer to the question.

Those are just personal opinions that are irrelevant and lead to false conclusions. We see Jesus cut through this type of stuff to get to the heart of the matter: "*But who do **you** say that I am?*"

The road to destruction is wide. Some will reject the notion that Jesus, the man, ever existed and consider Him a fib; an outright lie. Others will disregard virtually everything known about Jesus and paint Him as simply a man, no more and no less; just a man who has been dead for nearly 2,000 years. But some will answer as the Apostle Peter did...

*"Simon Peter answered and said, '**You are the Christ,
the Son of the living God.**' Jesus answered and said
to him, '**Blessed are you, Simon, son of Jonah, for
flesh and blood has not revealed this to you, but
My Father who is in heaven.**'"* [1]

Blessed are those who know the truth! It's a blessing because the understanding comes from God. In other words, it's not a human accomplishment. God has revealed the truth to those who believe.

Being that you're conscious and reading this book, I'm working on the assumption that you're alive. And if there is still breath in your lungs, you still have time to turn things around. If you've not yet put your full belief in Jesus, I encourage you to pray right now. It doesn't need to be something fancy, just ask God to open your heart to understand His truth. Ask that He would give you ears to hear and eyes to see. Ask that He would bless you that you would believe. And don't wait. Do it right now, friend. I'm not going anywhere. Take your time.

I'm praying for you, too. I'm praying that you would believe so you can build your life on the solid rock; on the Chief Cornerstone that is Jesus Christ. Nothing else will do.

*"Therefore, everyone who hears these words of mine and
puts them into practice is like a wise man who built his
house on the rock. The rain came down, the streams rose,*

---

1. Matthew 16:16-17

and the winds blew and beat against the house; yet, it did not fall, because it had its foundation on the rock. But everyone who hears these words of mine and does not put them into practice is like a foolish man who built his house on sand. The rain came down, the streams rose, and the winds blew and beat against that house, and it fell with a great crash. When Jesus had finished saying these things, the crowds were amazed at His teaching, because He taught as one who had authority, and not as their teachers of the law."[2]

Your career... sand. Your reputation... sand. Your accomplishments... sand. Being a godless "good person" ... sand. The stock market... sand. Politics... quicksand. I think you get the idea. These things aren't inherently bad. They're part of life. But if any one of them is #1 in your life before Jesus, you're truly missing the entire point.

I know this because I've been there. I appeared to have it all: a beautiful wife, beautiful kids, wonderful family, great job, nice house, friendly demeanor, etc. Yet, I was spiritually broke. Sure, I went to church on most Sundays, but God was nowhere near first place in my life. I was a passive spectator, not an active participating committed member of the church. God certainly wasn't my top priority or focus in life. I acknowledged God, but I felt like I personally was the biggest reason for my success. Oh, how wrong I was! I'm grateful to God for allowing pain into my life to shatter the foolish illusion that I was in control.

---

2. Matthew 7:24-28

At some point, we all look in the mirror and realize how far from perfect we are. The fact that every one of us is a sinner should be the most obvious thing imaginable. The Good News is that there is no condemnation, but only eternal life and everlasting joy awaiting those who believe in Jesus! We must be born again to truly be alive.

> *"All of us also lived among them at one time, gratifying the cravings of our flesh and following its desires and thoughts. Like the rest, we were by nature, deserving of wrath. But because of his great love for us, God, who is rich in mercy, made us alive with Christ even when we were dead in transgressions – it is by grace you have been saved."* [3]

You are not damaged goods, friend. You're just like every other person on the planet – a sinner, by nature, who deserves the wrath of God. But... if Jesus rose from the dead, Christianity is true. And as mind-blowing as that sounds, we can't shake the undeniable historical F.A.C.T.S. [4]

This actual historical event is the structural integrity of our faith. When we build our faith upon the Chief Cornerstone, no winds of life can destroy it. So, I declare to you today:

---

3. Ephesians 2:3-5

4. Derived from Dr. Gary Habermas' Minimal Facts Argument.

I choose to believe Jesus rose from the dead due to F.A.C.T.S. Therefore, Jesus proved He is who He said He is, the Son of God.

Since Jesus is the Son of God, my view of the Bible is based on what <u>He</u> taught about it. He taught that the Bible is the authoritative Word of God. Therefore, my #1 priority is to live in agreement with what it says.

What it says is, absolutely no sin can exist in heaven, but absolutely every person on Earth is a sinner. The Good News is, Jesus willingly suffered, died, and rose again to remove the sins of believers. Therefore, I've ditched all my own efforts and put my belief in Jesus alone as the solution.

I put my belief in Jesus alone because He said, "I am <u>the way</u>, the truth, and the life. No one comes to the Father except through me." Therefore, the single most loving thing I can do for someone else is to share with them the Good News.

I share the Good News not by any human authority, but as an ambassador for the one true living God. He exists eternally in three persons — The Father, The Son, and The Holy Spirit. Therefore, as ambassador, I demolish every objection and every proud thing that sets itself up against the truth of God.

The truth of God is Jesus. He's building His church, and nothing can overcome it. Therefore, being an active member of my church is how I live my life.

My life has been made new. I know God loves me because He didn't leave me the way He found me. Therefore, you can choose for yourself who you will serve, but as for me and my house, we will serve the Lord.

You know where I stand. What say you, friend? **Fib, Dead, or God?**

***

DECLARATION OF FAITH

Y ou know I wouldn't leave you hanging!

In case you didn't download the *Fib, Dead, or God?*
F.A.C.T.S. Sheet earlier, you can get it here.

It's printable and shareable, and it contains the entire declaration of faith we've built throughout this book.

TURN THE PAGE FOR MORE!

JAMES FINKE READERS' CLUB

My free monthly email newsletter is packed with useful info to help you share the Good News of Jesus Christ with others. It contains deals and giveaways that aren't offered anywhere else, and you'll be the first to hear when new books in the series are released!

Subscribers receive a welcome package that includes:

1. A free book of mine that is ONLY available to my readers' club.

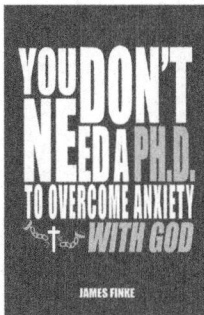

2. A free audio download of the "You Don't Need a Ph.D. to Find G-O-D" message I delivered at my home church.

CLICK HERE TO SUBSCRIBE

MORE BOOKS BY JAMES FINKE

Have you read the entire *CHRISTIANITY UN-COMPLICATED* SERIES?

This book distills and deciphers the evidence that the God of the Bible exists. Are you ready? Let's talk God.

***

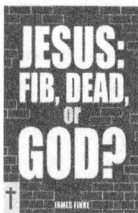

This book answers the most important question in history, asked by the most important person in history. Are you ready? Let's talk Jesus.

***

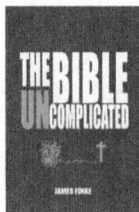

This book gives the business case for why we believe the Bible is the Word of God. Are you ready? Let's talk Bible.

***

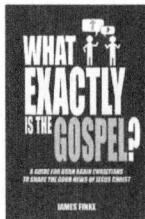

This book shares the most powerful message ever delivered on planet Earth. Let's talk Gospel.

Please enjoy this sneak preview of book #3 in the series...

INTRODUCTION

I'm in the business of taking risk. Calculated risk. No, I'm not a poker player, a tightrope walker, or some sort of breathtaking acrobat at the circus. For fifteen years, I've worked as a Professional Liability Insurance Underwriter. We cover professionals against lawsuits that claim they made a mistake in performing their services. This is known as "errors and omissions" insurance, or E&O.

If that seems anticlimactic to you, you're in good company. It's the type of profession that almost invariably triggers a blank stare when brought up in conversation. But underwriters like me spend their days assessing risk and making multi-million-dollar bets based on that research.

The term "underwriter" is said to have been coined in the 17th century at the world-famous Lloyds Coffee Shop in London. This coffee shop was frequented by many in the shipping industry and became the go-to location to obtain marine insurance. Risk-takers would literally write their name under the total amount of risk they were willing to accept for a specified fee. Hence, underwriter.

Then and now, the stakes can be very high. I specialize in underwriting companies that have, in their past, been sued for hundreds of thousands or millions of dollars. The reality is that even experts in their field make mistakes. It's not unusual for us to see a professional who is being sued for the first time in a stellar 30+ year career.

What's more, a company doesn't even necessarily need to have made a mistake to be sued. An old adage in our business is "all it takes is an unhappy client for a claim." For example, divorce attorneys get sued for negligence constantly – much more so than attorneys practicing other types of law. Are divorce attorneys a particularly negligent bunch? Do they make up the "C's get degrees" crowd at law schools? Of course not. The issue is that, almost by definition, the people hiring divorce attorneys are unhappy. Unhappy clients often sue their practitioners, especially professionals involved in nasty family disputes.

It's not glamorous, but business insurance like E&O is essential for a healthy economy. This is because we agree to take on a company's financial risk in exchange for a fee. Absent this risk transfer, companies would constantly be a lawsuit away from disaster. Indeed, even if a suit is dismissed in your favor, it could easily cost 5, 6, or 7 figures to defend. And that's when you know what you're doing.

Most don't. Nor should they. As an example, architects are in the business of providing design services, not the business of defending negligence lawsuits. They need counsel. In addition to the promise to pay from the insurance company, professionals who buy an insurance policy are enlisting our expert defense services. They benefit by retaining an insurance company with expert claims analysts who, in turn, maintain relationships with expert defense counsel law firms.

Underwriters utilize complex criteria to evaluate the many risk factors at play within a company. Technology continues to produce better tools for this assessment. Still, there remains a human element, particularly for higher-hazard risks such as what I handle. So there's an art and a science to underwriting. At the end of the day, we're trying to determine the odds this professional will make a mistake and how severe might the consequences be if they do.

The probability that a professional will make a mistake is reflected in their claim "frequency." How frequently are they sued? Obviously, we're trying to pick "winners," who are the least likely to make mistakes and have an issue. That said, we go into it knowing that no matter how diligent, some of the companies we choose to cover will get sued. That's why we must consider the other side of the coin—how bad might the downside be if the firm does indeed make a mistake? This is called claims severity – i.e., how severe will the loss be? For example, if Mainstreet Accounting firm makes an error on the taxes of an individual who earns $35,000 a year, it would take a relatively small sum to make that client whole again. But if a big shot accounting firm messes up an audit of a publicly-traded company, the mistake could cost millions.

That's severity. And for risks that have a particularly severe potential downside, underwriters may be less likely to go "all-in" on covering them. For example, suppose I'm evaluating a structural engineer who is responsible for the safety of bridges. In that case, I may not be willing to provide a huge sum of insurance for their services. Though it's unlikely they'll have a problem, the results could be catastrophic if they do. So, naturally, I'd want to limit my downside exposure in case it did.

I've wagered hundreds of millions of dollars on behalf of my employers throughout my career. These are calculated bets based on the meticulous evaluation of risk factors, and we've consistently produced a profit. But, perhaps even more important than the companies we've chosen to cover are the companies we've decided not to cover. If we lack confidence in a company, we may not participate or may only be willing to make a small wager until the company has proven itself.

In addition to the individual company assessments, we work diligently to maintain a broad and balanced portfolio. We're constantly monitoring our downside and ensuring we're not too heavily concentrated in any area. We spread our risk across various professions, various geographic regions, various broker partners, various products, and much more. The whole idea is that we don't want any single deal to be able to sink us if it goes wrong.

With all of this in mind, it may surprise you to know that I've gone all-in and wagered everything on the Bible. Everything. My life is organized around it, and I've staked my eternity on the fact that it's true. In fact, billions of Christians have done so and continue to do so every day. This is because we believe that the Bible truly is the authoritative word of God.

So how does an analytical, risk-assessing, spreadsheet-loving insurance underwriter come to this conclusion? It's a reasonable question to ask, and we will walk through it together. The beautiful thing is, when something is correct, you can assess a wide range of factors, and they will all point to the truth. We'll look at how important the Bible is to the Christian faith and why we believe it's true. I'll provide you with some easy-to-remember information to help bolster your faith in a skeptical world. And we'll even dispose of some pesky, weak excuses that unbelievers lean on like, "I can't believe the Bible because it's been translated so many times."

Are you ready? Let's talk about why we believe the Bible.

To continue reading, purchase here:

AMAZON US

AMAZON UK

AMAZON CA

AMAZON AUS

REVIEW REQUEST

If you enjoyed *Jesus: Fib, Dead, or God?*, I'd sincerely appreciate it if you'd leave a review. Positive reviews, even if just a sentence or two, are a huge help to search results and credibility so other people can find this book. Thank you!

Review Amazon US.

Review Amazon Canada.

Review Amazon UK.

Review Amazon Australia

God Bless!

ABOUT THE AUTHOR

James Finke has spent the past 15+ years in Corporate America managing $50-million-dollar insurance portfolios. He is an expert in assessing risk and hedging bets. Therefore, it sometimes catches people off-guard when they discover he has gone all-in and wagered *everything* that the Bible is true.

His writing ministry began as a "quarantine project" for his church back in 2020. It has developed into a book series in 17 countries and counting. The ultimate goal of the ministry is to glorify God and share the Gospel. Therefore, 100% of book proceeds are poured right back into the ministry.

James lives with his wife and four young kids in Connecticut. Follow James on Instagram, Facebook, and TikTok.

Printed in Great Britain
by Amazon